THE ACCELERATING DECLINE IN AMERICA'S HIGH-SKILLED WORKFORCE: Implications for Immigration Policy

Jacob Funk Kirkegaard

PETERSON INSTITUTE FOR INTERNATIONAL ECONOMICS
Washington, DC
December 2007

Jacob Funk Kirkegaard has been a research associate at the Peterson Institute since 2002. Before joining the Institute, he worked with the Danish Ministry of Defense, the United Nations in Iraq, and in the private financial sector. He is a graduate of the Danish Army's Special School of Intelligence and Linguistics with the rank of first lieutenant; the University of Aarhus in Aarhus, Denmark; and Columbia University in New York.

He is the coauthor of *Transforming the European Economy* (2004) and *Pension Reforms in Rich Countries under Demographic Stress* (forthcoming) and assisted with *Accelerating the Globalization of America: The Role for Information Technology* (2006). His current research focuses on European economies and reform, pension systems and accounting rules, demographics, offshoring, high-skilled immigration, and the impact of information technology.

PETER G. PETERSON INSTITUTE FOR INTERNATIONAL ECONOMICS
1750 Massachusetts Avenue, NW
Washington, DC 20036-1903
(202) 328-9000   FAX: (202) 659-3225
www.petersoninstitute.org

C. Fred Bergsten, *Director*
Edward Tureen, *Director of Publications, Marketing, and Web Development*

Typesetting by Marla Banov
Printing by Kirby Lithographic Company, Inc.

For reprints/permission to photocopy please contact the APS customer service department at Copyright Clearance Center, Inc., 222 Rosewood Drive, Danvers, MA 01923; or email requests to: info@copyright.com

Printed in the United States of America
10 09 08   5 4 3 2 1

Library of Congress Cataloging-in-Publication Data

Kirkegaard, Jacob F.
    Accelerating decline in America's high-skilled workforce : implications for immigration policy / Jacob Kirkegaard.
        p. cm.
    Includes bibliographical references and index.
        ISBN 978-0-88132-413-6 (alk. paper)
    1. United States--Emigration and immigration--Government policy. 2. Skilled labor--United States. I. Title.

JV6483.K58 2007
325.73--dc22   2007042352

THE ACCELERATING DECLINE IN AMERICA'S HIGH-SKILLED WORKFORCE:
Implications for Immigration Policy

Contents

Boxes

Preface

Immigration has become an increasingly important issue on the global economic agenda while invariably remaining a domestically contested political issue. Regrettably, the recent debate in the United States on immigration reform has failed to pay sufficient attention to several accelerating trends in immigration of high-skilled workers. US policymakers need to acknowledge these trends before they produce an emergency.

America rose to economic prominence during the 20th century on the shoulders of the most highly skilled workforce in the global economy. However, during the last 30 years the hitherto constant skill improvement of the US workforce has stagnated: Americans aged 25–34 today do not possess noticeably higher skills than do their soon-to-retire baby boomer parents.

Meanwhile, skill improvement in labor forces in many other advanced countries has surpassed that in the US labor force. While a large share of Americans aged 55 and over had upon their entry into the US labor force acquired the key to success in the global service-oriented economy—tertiary education—today's American labor force entrants barely make the global top 10, and relatively more high-skilled Americans will soon pass into retirement than in any other country. The United States thus risks losing its status as the most skill abundant country in the global economy.

Successful implementation of education policies will produce more high-skilled American workers only in the long term. In the short to medium term, America will increasingly require foreign high-skilled workers and will therefore have to reform its high-skilled immigration policies and processes not only to welcome the best and the brightest but also to make it easier for them to stay.

Other rich nations, traditionally less open to immigration than the United States, have in recent years embraced policies to "manage" immigration and have become far more open to high-skilled immigrants than before. As a result, the United States is increasingly becoming just one of many possible destinations for high-skilled immigrants.

Against this backdrop, Jacob F. Kirkegaard's study provides a detailed analysis of the present but unreformed and increasingly dysfunctional US high-skilled immigration system. Fortunately for US high-skilled immigration reform efforts, however, this study verifies that concerns for the plight of American high-skilled workers in the face of significant inflows of foreign high-skilled workers are unfounded. Kirkegaard investigates empirically the labor-market situation faced by US software workers—usually depicted in the US media as the group facing the greatest risks from globalization—and reveals that these occupations enjoy full employment at record levels in today's US economy.

Based on these findings, Kirkegaard offers a coherent package of proposals to reform the US high-skilled immigration system. The aim of these reform proposals is to facilitate continued large inflows of high-skilled workers to the United States in a manner that enjoys broad domestic political support.

The Peter G. Peterson Institute for International Economics is a private, nonprofit institution for the study and discussion of international economic policy. Its purpose is to analyze important issues in that area and to develop and communicate practical new approaches for dealing with them. The Institute is completely nonpartisan.

The Institute is funded by a highly diversified group of philanthropic foundations, private corporations, and interested individuals. About 30 percent of the Institute's resources in our latest fiscal year were provided by contributors outside the United States, including about 12 percent from Japan.

The Institute's Board of Directors bears overall responsibilities for the Institute and gives general guidance and approval to its research program, including the identification of topics that are likely to become important over the medium run (one to three years) and that should be addressed by the Institute. The director, working closely with the staff and outside Advisory Committee, is responsible for the development of particular projects and makes the final decision to publish an individual study.

The Institute hopes that its studies and other activities will contribute to building a stronger foundation for international economic policy around the world. We invite readers of these publications to let us know how they think we can best accomplish this objective.

C. FRED BERGSTEN
Director
November 2007

Acknowledgments

This policy analysis benefited from the input of many of my colleagues at the Peterson Institute. I would particularly like to thank C. Fred Bergsten, Madona Devasahayam, Catherine L. Mann, Arvind Subramanian, and Ed Tureen for their many thoughtful contributions.

Introduction

America was indebted to immigration for her settlement and prosperity.
That part of America which had encouraged them most
had advanced most rapidly in population, agriculture and the arts.

—James Madison (1751–1836)[1]

The high-skilled immigration system in the United States is in desperate
need of reform.[2] While comprehensive immigration policy made it back
onto the US political agenda in the summer of 2007, regrettably little attention is being paid to visa policies and procedures for high-skilled foreign
workers, some of which are increasingly becoming arbitrary, time con-
suming, and costly.

The entire annual H-1B temporary work visa quota available to US
businesses was snapped up in less than one day in early April 2007 and,
due to oversubscription, had to be allocated based on a random lottery
(see chapter 3). And as recently as July 2007, rapidly changing and conflicting US governmental policy decisions on who can file for legal permanent resident ("green card") status and when confounded sponsoring US
employers and high-skilled foreigners working here on temporary visas
while waiting for years to adjust their status to permanent residents. The

---

*Jacob Funk Kirkegaard is currently residing in the United States on an H-1B visa sponsored by the
Peterson Institute for International Economics, which is also sponsoring his pending adjustment of
status to legal permanent resident (green card). He is a Danish national, and none of the reforms to
the US high-skilled immigration system proposed in this policy analysis will affect his personal situation.*

1. The Debates in the Federal Convention of 1787, August 13.

2. "High-skilled" in this policy analysis, unless otherwise indicated, refers to persons with at
least tertiary education—i.e., the equivalent of a four-year college degree or higher.

far-reaching policy decisions were subsequently clarified and partly reversed, but the debacle has undoubtedly lowered foreign workers' confidence in the system and their hope for a permanent future in the United States by significantly adding to the delay in processing of pending applications (see chapter 2).

It must be acknowledged at the outset, however, that historically the US high-skilled immigration system has in many ways been the world's leading such system and retains several well-functioning programs, but its present shortcomings have become increasingly pronounced in the main temporary work visa, the H-1B, and the legal permanent resident programs (see chapter 2). The two programs play a substantial role in bringing in foreign high-skilled workers and permanently keeping them here and could play an even bigger role as demand for high-skilled workers in the US economy increases.

The lack of a serious push to reform these programs is unfortunate because America is in the midst of a transition from its historical position at the pinnacle of the global skills hierarchy to a position where it is struggling to remain even in the world's top 10. This policy analysis presents evidence that in the coming decade, America will face substantial and broad skill shortages and will therefore have to remain attractive to "the best and the brightest."

The long-term economic growth of an advanced country like the United States in the age of rapid globalization is with certainty highly correlated with the skill level of its residents. This is the fundamental insight of growth theory provided by Robert Solow in the 1950s. The skill level in turn depends heavily on both the education and immigration policies of the country.

The combined outcome of these policies is a ready supply of high-skilled workers, which is critical for globally competing businesses. Domestic education policies—for the purposes of this policy analysis, policies that enable a country's young people to get a university degree—are clearly more important because they affect far more people than do immigration policies. The main reason for focusing on tertiary education in this policy analysis is the assertion that this skill level is most required to "learn how to learn." Tertiary skills are the crucial stepping stones to a flexible, fluctuating, and increasingly services-oriented global economy.

The principal objective of any government must be the welfare of its own population, so when considering the overall public response to an increased demand for high-skilled workers, domestic education policies will always retain primacy over immigration policies (which invariably benefit the populations of other countries, as they would otherwise not choose to emigrate).[3] Immigration should not become a substitute for edu-

---

3. It will be a laudable goal for a destination country's immigration policies to seek to pro-

cation of the domestic population—the latter, however, is a topic well outside the scope of this policy analysis.

That said, any reform of a country's education system inevitably takes considerable time—likely decades—to have a discernible effect on the skill level of the workforce. It is, for instance, well established that many of the positive economic effects on the US economy of the 1944 GI Bill emerged only many years later.[4] As such, from the perspective of finding a problem-solving policy tool for the short and medium terms, high-skilled immigration policies in a high-wage country like the United States, which (in theory at least) can be altered relatively quickly and have a more immediate impact on a country's supply of high-skilled workers, should be at least partly responsive to the long-term outcome of that same country's domestic education policies. In other words, education policy is a fait accompli, whose long-term economic impact policymakers designing high-skilled immigration policies must never ignore.

Large increases in a country's domestic output of university graduates will, ceteris paribus, reduce the demand from businesses and other employers for high-skilled foreign workers. On the other hand, stagnating output of domestic university graduates will, ceteris paribus, increase the demand for foreign university graduates and put pressure on high-skilled immigration regulation to facilitate this demand. The latter case is of particular relevance, because—as many economists have established—the US economy has during the last decades been experiencing skill-biased technological change, which has raised the relative demand for high-skilled workers in the US economy.[5]

Before proceeding with the analysis, it is useful to consider why high-skilled immigration is different from immigration in general. A country's overall immigration system serves multiple purposes: upholding sovereignty and border control, national security (including aiding local employees working for military forces deployed overseas[6]), and long-held

mote the welfare of origin countries too. Whether this is on balance the case is a complicated matter beyond the scope of this policy analysis. However, it is most useful to conceptualize high-skilled immigration as exchange-oriented "brain flows" between different countries, rather than zero-sum "brain drains."

4. Officially titled the Servicemen's Readjustment Act of 1944, the 1944 GI Bill provided returning World War II veterans (commonly referred to as GIs) with college or vocational education as well as one year of unemployment compensation. For its positive impact on the US economy, see, for instance, Bound and Turner (2002) and Eggertsson (1972).

5. There is a vast literature on this subject. For a recent exhaustive overview, see Feenstra (2000); Levy and Temin (2007); Levy and Murnane (1992); Autor, Levy, and Murnane (2001); and Mann (2003, 2006).

6. The current debate on making US visas available to local employees of coalition forces in Iraq—interpreter/translator applicants until recently faced a nine-year waiting period—is another example of the many unintended but potentially highly damaging spillover effects into other policy areas of the current broad-based deadlock on US immigration policy reform. See "Envoy Urges Visas for Iraqis Aiding U.S.," *Washington Post*, July 22, 2007, A1.

legal and humanitarian traditions, while reflecting national identity politics, for instance. This exhaustive set of priorities, however, is not relevant for the part of the immigration system that concerns high-skilled foreign workers. A sensible high-skilled immigration system involves itself first and foremost with a country's economic growth prospects and should generally aim to appropriately align two traditional "welfare economics" issues, namely enabling a country's employers and businesses to recruit needed high-skilled workers if necessary also from abroad (efficiency) while preserving the interests of the resident workforce (equity).

It would be fortuitous if high-skilled immigration policies in America were reformed as part of a "grand compromise" on immigration encom- passing all the different purposes listed above. But it should be clear to all stakeholders that in the event such a "grand compromise" is not politically possible, then holding much-needed high-skilled immigration reforms hostage as a political negotiating strategy puts continuing US economic growth at risk. If US-located businesses cannot get the high-skilled employees they need to get their work done inside the United States, then they will as a matter of simple competitive logic in a global economy be increasingly likely to shift jobs and workplaces to locations outside US borders, where they will have progressively better access to the workers they require. A recent survey by the National Venture Capital Association (2007, 24) of privately held venture capital–backed US companies shows that restrictive US high-skilled immigration laws had influenced the decisions of one-third of such companies to place more personnel at facilities abroad.[7] To reestablish its leadership in global talent, in the short run America will have to revamp its high-skilled immigration policies and processes to not only welcome more highly skilled foreign workers but also make it easier for them to stay.

This policy analysis first shows how America will increasingly require high-skilled foreign workers to buttress its aging skilled workforce and will do so precisely at a time when many other Organization for Economic Cooperation and Development (OECD) countries are reforming their high-skilled immigration regulation to attract highly sought global talent. Second, it focuses on the H-1B and L-1 visa and green card programs to illustrate how the current high-skilled immigration system is characterized by a dual trend: volatile expansion in numbers concerning Indian nationals but relative stability concerning other foreigners. Third, it addresses the welfare trade-off between economic efficiency and worker interests, looks more closely at the labor-market conditions faced by those Americans most affected by high-skilled immigration—software workers—and addresses ways in which immigration policy can best match foreign workers to US employers. Finally, it presents a package of coherent and parsimonious reforms of present US high-skilled immigration laws.

---

7. The study singles out the lack of H-1B visas as the major human resources bottleneck.

High-Skilled Workers: Stagnating in the United States, Rising Fast in Other Countries?

It's not what we don't know that gives us trouble. It's what we know that ain't so.

—Will Rogers

The US labor force is highly diverse and dynamic. Yet, intuitively, its long-term average skill level is principally determined by the relative magnitudes of labor-market entries by young workers upon finishing their initial education and exits by retiring older workers.[1] The United States led the world in education throughout the 20th century and benefited greatly from it. It is well known that a country reaps a demographic dividend from quantitatively large young population cohorts entering the workforce.[2] Similarly, in countries like the United States, a positive economic effect has also been felt from the long-term qualitative improvement in the US labor force with less-skilled workers retiring and more high-skilled workers entering the workforce.

---

1. The long-term trend is the focus of the first section. Therefore, among many things, it ignores the compositional effects of cyclical changes in hours worked among different groups of workers, as well as the "effective skill effects" from rising levels of experience and continuous lifelong work-related training. Some of these data (in the form of the labor composition index) are compiled annually by the Bureau of Labor Statistics (BLS 2007) for use in computing private business-sector multifactor productivity (MFP). Such "effective skill effects" arise when firms in economic trouble, for instance, lay off workers with least seniority first or blue collar workers ahead of white collar professionals. See also OECD (2007a, 62ff) for a review of the productivity effects of lifelong learning programs in the OECD countries.

2. For a recent overview of this literature, see International Monetary Fund's *Finance and Development*, September 2006.

Many researchers have empirically found such gains to long-term US economic growth from rising skill levels using different methodologies. J. Bradford DeLong, Claudia Goldin, and Lawrence F. Katz (2003) estimate that the combined direct and indirect effects (via research and development and multifactor productivity [MFP]) of rising skill levels in the labor force were the single largest contributor to US economic growth in the 20th century. Other researchers find that an additional year of schooling raises GDP per capita by up to 5 percent and MFP by up to 0.9 percent.[3]

However, this era of broadly rising skill levels in the US labor force is drawing to a close here early in the 21st century. A frequently overlooked side-effect of the imminent retirement of the generally well-educated baby boomer generation is that their retirement will soon take as many high-skilled people out of the US labor force as will simultaneously enter it. This novel development is illustrated in figure 1.1.[4]

Size and Educational Attainment of Resident US Population

Figure 1.1 shows the detailed educational attainment of the resident US population[5] by five-year age cohort, starting from the age group when people will usually have completed their bachelor's degree (25–29 years) to the age group when they are deep into retirement (age 75+).[6] It is important to

---

3. OECD (2007a). See also Bassanini and Scarpetta (2001), Cohen and Soto (2007), de la Fuente and Ciccone (2003), and Splitz-Oener (2007).

4. The underlying data for figure 1.1 are presented in more detail in table A.1 in the statistical appendix.

5. These data are from the Bureau of Labor Statistics and the Census Bureau's Current Population Survey, which samples random US households and makes no distinction between US citizens and resident aliens.

6. These data are a snapshot in time and when used here as a "de facto time-series" incorporate the combined share effects of at least four effects active over time: domestic US education (highest level of education attained by Americans in different age groups), immigration (are new immigrants of all ages high or low skilled? For most of the answer, see figure 1.5), lifelong learning (people may choose to go back to school at an older age), and mortality differentials (highly educated people generally live longer than less-educated people). Disentangling these individual effects in detail is, however, beyond the scope of this policy analysis. But these effects work in different directions and therefore do not materially impact the conclusions drawn here. It must be emphasized, though, that lifelong learning is likely less of an uncertainty than many people think, when considering whether people "jump" to one of the higher educational attainment meta-groups depicted in figure 1.1. Usually, lifelong skill acquisition entails acquiring more hands-on skills directly needed to perform a particular job and does not lead to the crossing of educational thresholds into one of the other meta-groups listed in figure 1.1. Most people who do acquire another degree later in life already have a bachelor's or master's degree and therefore do not add to the headcount of the highly skilled by going back to school. Conversation with Barbara Ischinger, director of the OECD Education Directorate, September 18, 2007, at the launch of the *Education at a Glance 2007:*

Figure 1.1   US educational attainment (highest level attained), 2006

percent share of age group

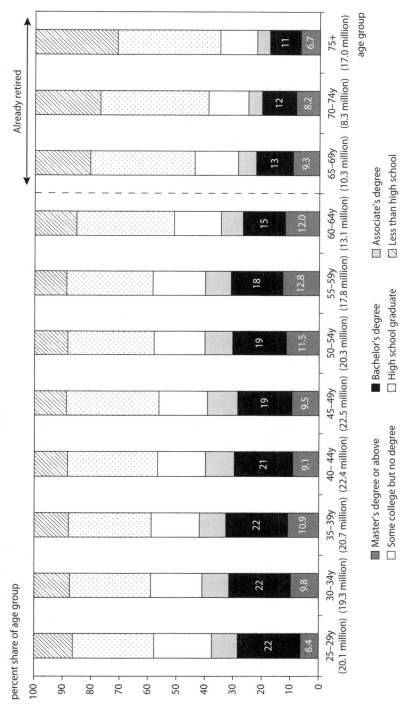

Source: Bureau of Labor Statistics and Census Bureau, Current Population Survey, 2006 Annual Social and Economic Supplement, available at www.bls.gov/cps.

note that figure 1.1 implicitly assumes "fixed thresholds" for entering each category. Hence it assumes, for instance, that a 25–29 year old required the same skill level to get a high school degree as did a 75+ year old.[7]

Figure 1.1 conveys at least two important points: First, the average skill level of the US workforce saw continued improvements up until the time those now aged 55–59 entered the workforce—i.e., until the mid- to late 1970s. The share of unskilled workers (i.e., those with less than a high school degree) declined rapidly, while the number of university graduates rose dramatically. Second, however, American residents aged 25–54 are generally not better educated than their immediately older fellow residents aged 55–59, indicating that the "demographic skills dividend" in the US workforce came to an end in the late 1970s.

Fortunately, the full economic impact of this approximately 30-year stagnation in the average skill level of the US population—covering the resident population from age 25–29 years to 55–59 years—has been delayed until now,[8] as the average skill levels of retiring cohorts aged 65+ have hitherto been below those of younger generations entering the labor force.[9] However, within the next decade, this trend will by and large cease because the 55–59 year olds are just as well educated as today's labor-market entering "fully educated cohort" aged 30–34.[10] Indeed, as of 2006, there are more holders of master's, professional, and doctoral degrees among resident 55–59 year olds in America than there are among the 30–34 year olds.[11] In other words, unless the 30-year stagnation among advanced-de-

---

OECD Indicators publication at the National Education Association in Washington.

7. Some numeracy tests indicate that this assumption may be questionable, as they find evidence that the required level to graduate has declined over time. See, for instance, the 2003 *Trends in International Mathematics and Science Study* (NCES 2004) or the adult literacy survey in OECD/Statistics Canada (2005).

8. Indeed the National Science Foundation in 2005 almost triumphantly announced that the total number of individuals in the United States with at least a college degree rose more than 40 percent from 1993 to 2003—from 29 million to 41 million. This number, however, fails to take into account the rising US total population (up 13 percent from 1993 to 2003) and the rising average age of US degree holders. See National Science Foundation (2005).

9. US labor force participation for the age group 60–64 in 2006 was 52.5 percent but only 29 percent for the age group 65–69, 17 percent for the age group 70–74, and 6.4 percent for the 75+ group. Total labor force participation for the 16+ age group was 66.2 percent. Despite gradually rising Social Security retirement ages, it thus remains accurate to state that Americans on average retire around age 65. The OECD estimates the effective (i.e., taking into account all early retirement programs) age of withdrawal from the US labor force at about 64 years (Bureau of Labor Statistics and Census Bureau, Current Population Survey; and OECD 2006a).

10. "Fully educated" indicates that people usually will not have finished their master's, professional, or doctoral degrees until reaching the age cohort of 30–34. As such, an educational improvement in the 25–29 age cohort of bachelor's degree holders should be expected.

11. In 2006 there were 1.61 million master's degree holders, 305,000 professional degree hold-

gree holders in the resident American population is quickly reversed, a depletion of the graduate degree–holding US workforce seems both imminent and unavoidable.

Given the fundamental economic relationship between supply, demand, and prices, such a scenario will invariably cause earnings inequality between those with high levels (at least a college degree) and those with low levels of education in America to start rising again in the near future.[12] However, as has been the case so far, any additional widening of the wage distribution will not be due to the fact that the US labor force is simply not adjusting fast enough to rising demand for high-skilled workers from technological innovation and international trade. It will be because the US labor force will soon have largely stopped adjusting at all!

The stagnating skills acquisition in the US workforce shown in figure 1.1 can also be described by projecting the share of the total population that can be expected to have acquired tertiary education in the coming decades, given the skill level of those already above age 25 in 2006. This exercise allows for reasonable projections for at least as long as the age groups surveyed in 2006 remain in the population.[13] The US Census Bureau has since 1940 regularly estimated the share of the US population aged 25 and above with at least a four-year college education. These data for select years from 1940 to 2006, as well as projections until 2035, are presented in figure 1.2.[14] However, given that high-skilled people also can be expected to live considerable parts of their lives in retirement, it is useful to consider the share of the "US workforce" that through time has attained tertiary education. Figure 1.2 illustrates this point with the age group 25–64. US

---

ers, and 349,000 doctoral degree holders aged 55–59 in America, while there were 1.4 million master's degree holders, 281,000 professional degree holders, and 199,000 doctoral degree holders aged 30–34. See table A.1 in the statistical appendix. Auriol (2007) also presents data showing that of six out of seven surveyed countries—Canada, Argentina, Germany, Australia, and Switzerland—the United States has the oldest PhD population on average, with doctoral degree holders from Portugal being older.

12. The Economic Policy Institute (EPI) estimates that the wage premium for college relative to high school graduates reached 47.1 percent in 2005. This wage premium, however, has been essentially stagnant since 1995, when it reached 46.7 percent, which was preceded by an increase from less than 30 percent in the late 1970s. See EPI datazone at www.epi.org/datazone/06. See also Lawrence (forthcoming).

13. The projection methodology used here assumes that the educational attainment of age groups 25–29 and 30–34 will be retained throughout the projection period, such that the 2006 share of the 30–34 age group will be held constant into the future as older age groups surveyed in 2006 exit the relevant age group. Individual age groups are then weighted by their share of the total relevant age group population total. Note that no adjustment is made for differences in mortality rates among people of different educational attainment, immigration, or lifelong learning in these projections.

14. By 2035 the age group 30–34 surveyed in 2006 will have passed into the oldest 75+ age group, and the projections become flat by assumption thereafter.

Figure 1.2 Share of the US workforce with at least tertiary education, 1940–2035

percent share of total population
in age group

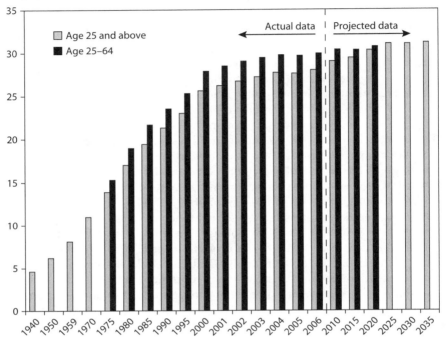

Sources: Bureau of Labor Statistics and Census Bureau, Current Population Survey, available at www.bls.gov/cps; author's calculations.

Census data at this level of age detail go back only to the mid-1970s, so there is not enough information to project this age group beyond 2020.

Two distinct trends are visible in figure 1.2: First, the rapid rise in the share of the US population aged 25 and above that had attained tertiary education started slowing dramatically just after 2000 and will slow even further going forward. Second, part of this continued slower rise after 2006 comes from the continued rise in the share of highly skilled people over 65. By about 2020, Americans 65 years and above—the overwhelming majority of whom will be in retirement—will be about as well educated as the US workforce in the 25–64 age group, the usual workforce age range.
To retain this group of elderly high-skilled Americans in the workforce in coming decades poses a significant challenge.[15]

---

15. For the labor-market challenge of aging high-skilled populations, see also Baily and Kirkegaard (forthcoming).

If one takes "equal opportunity for all" in America seriously and believes that every American truly has access to as much education as he or she demands and desires, then this observed stagnation in skill levels at late 1970s levels would point to a "revealed preference" and likely to a resulting maximum skills capacity of the resident US population. This stagnation would again indicate that it occurred near the pinnacle of what a large population like America's can realistically achieve, assuming that everyone finishes as much education as he or she individually desires. After all, not everyone can possibly graduate from university.

If this indeed were the case, then one would not need to lose too much sleep over this stagnation, as there would be no compelling reason to believe that populations in other rich countries would be able to do any better than potentially catch up with the overall US skill levels reached in the late 1970s. Alas, a look at internationally comparable statistics from the Organization for Economic Cooperation and Development (OECD) and the United Nations Educational, Scientific, and Cultural Organization (UNESCO) quickly dispels such notions.

Figure 1.3 presents a different calibration of internationally comparable "de facto time-series data" similar to those presented in figure 1.1 for the United States. The way to interpret figure 1.3 is to look at the difference (i.e., vertical distance) between the age groups. The larger the difference, the bigger the improvement in educational attainment among different age groups in the resident population—the 30-year time-series chronology in figure 1.3 goes "big square-circle-small square-big triangle." The countries are ranked by the educational attainment of age group 25–34.

It is important to note that no attempt is made in figure 1.3 to "adjust for quality differences" in tertiary educational experiences between countries. Of course, not every university around the globe is a Harvard, Stanford, Cambridge, or Indian Institute of Technology, so invariably considerable "skill aspects" are not included in figure 1.3. Such comparisons are significantly beyond the scope of this policy analysis. However, following the axiom that tertiary training is what principally enables individuals to quickly grasp new complex subjects and therefore makes it easier to train them on the (especially services-sector) job, it seems evident that in terms of describing the overall level of high-skilled workers in different countries' workforces, any impact of quality differences among universities will be swamped by the quantitative differences in tertiary skill uptake depicted in figure 1.3.[16]

Several things are clear from figure 1.3: First, Americans aged 55–64 by and large were the most highly skilled "free-market generation" of

---

16. See also data (presented later) on the share of foreign students at US universities. Their rising numbers further hamper any attempt to "adjust for quality differences" in university experiences between countries.

Figure 1.3 Share of population with tertiary education, by age, 2005

percent of age group

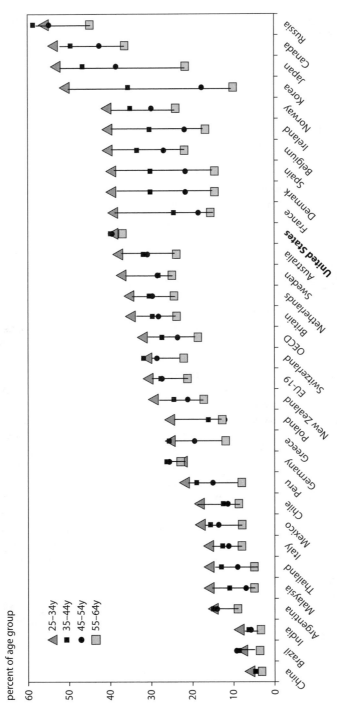

Legend:
- 25–34y
- 35–44y
- 45–54y
- 55–64y

Note: Tertiary education means at least a college degree. Data are for 2005 or latest available from 2003–04. The way to interpret this figure is to look at the difference (i.e., vertical distance) between the age groups. The larger the difference, the bigger the improvement in educational attainment among different age groups in the resident population—the 30-year time-series goes "big square-circle-small square-big triangle." The countries are ranked by educational attainment of age group 25–34.

Sources: UNESCO/OECD World Education Indicators; OECD (2007d); for China: National Bureau of Statistics of China (2005); for India: Ministry of Statistics and Programme Implementation (2005).

their time, beaten only by their Russian counterparts, who until 1991, from the perspective of competing workers, were "securely" imprisoned by the absurdities of communism and a centrally planned economy.[17] As such, no group in the world would have been in a better position to take advantage of trade liberalization and the opening up of global markets in the latter part of the 20th century than this group of Americans. There is little doubt that this erstwhile skill superiority of the US population has been the backbone of US political support for free trade in the 20th century (Scheve and Slaughter 2001). Stated in another way, up until and including the time when Americans aged 55–64 entered the labor force, America had, in Heckscher-Ohlin terms, abundant skilled labor among resident labor-market entrants relative to the rest of the world.[18]

Second, it is evident from figure 1.3 that the skill level expressed in terms of university education that America achieved in the late 1970s and has barely maintained since is not particularly impressive in the 21st century when compared with other countries. While the United States and Germany[19] are unique among OECD countries in having seen stagnating or declining average skill levels by this broad measure over all four age groups presented in figure 1.3, the educational attainment in many countries has continued from generational cohort to generational cohort in recent decades to soar past the levels achieved in the United States. Most impressive is South Korea, which has seen the share of university graduates among labor-market entrants rise from 10 to 50 percent in the approximately 30-year period captured in figure 1.3. Many other countries have also seen dramatic improvements—Japan, Canada, France, Spain, the Scandinavians, and Ireland are all at or significantly above the skill level found among US residents aged 25–34.

Moreover, it is noteworthy that while the average skill levels in Russia have stagnated in the last 20 years—which is not too surprising given the economic turmoil and crisis in the country—this stagnation has occurred at a much higher average skill level than in the United States (or Germany). As such, while their parents may have been "the brightest kids on the global trading block" when they entered the workforce, younger

17. On the other hand, the ability of a Soviet-style planned economy to "order" the production of a large number of university graduates should clearly not be underestimated.

18. The United States led the industrialized world in educational attainment from early in the 20th century; see Goldin (2001) and Goldin and Katz (2003). This supremacy was achieved by an education system that in the words of Goldin (2001, 3) was characterized by "public funding, openness, gender neutrality, local (and also state) control, separation of church and state, and an academic curriculum." See also Leamer (1984).

19. For a description of the dismal state of German university education, see, for instance, Burda (2006a, 2006b).

Americans today barely make the global top 10.[20] Simply put, America in the 21st century is no longer a skill-abundant country relative to an increasing share of the rest of the world.

Third, with the best-educated 55–64 year olds in the world, America faces an imminent disproportionately larger skills drain into retirement than other industrialized countries. Even if the skill levels of the resident workforce in, say, Canada or other countries with continuous improvements started stagnating today as they did in America in the late 1970s, it would still be about 30 years before they faced the same relative skill drain into retirement that America presently confronts. Should these countries find themselves in a similar situation (ignored so far by policymakers in Washington), they will have ample time for long-term reforms of their education system.

At least three issues emerge from the two trends in workforces described so far in this chapter—i.e., stagnating US university-degree skill levels since the late 1970s and accelerating relative decline versus other industrialized nations.[21] First, a relatively broad-based skills shortage in the United States extending significantly beyond the "usual suspect" fields of science and technology (see below) seems probable in the medium term. This shortage seems likely to accelerate already high US wage differentials between high- and low-skilled workers. The data in figure 1.1 thus should serve to allay many broader concerns about the labor-market situation facing high-skilled Americans in the coming decades.[22]

Second, the economics literature is fairly clear that skill levels overwhelmingly determine the attitudes of rich-world populations toward free trade[23]: High-skilled workers broadly favor free trade and vice versa. In light of the stagnation seen in US skill levels in the last 30 years, it is not surprising that age generally has little discernible effect on perceptions toward international trade.[24] However, one may speculate that the relative decline in skill levels among younger Americans versus their counterparts in other industrialized nations and developing economies like China

---

20. This is also reflected in the fact that in the late 1970s, 30 percent of the world's university students were in America; today that share has declined to 14 percent (NCEE 2007).

21. This accelerating decline arises from both a lower share of university degree holders among labor-market-entering cohorts and relatively higher numbers of university-trained retirees.

22. The US Census Bureau (2007, table 613) shows that the unemployment rate among college graduates has since 1992 consistently been more than 1 percent below that among nongraduates and always about or below 3 percent or essentially full employment.

23. See, for instance, Scheve and Slaughter (2001).

24. See, for instance, Scheve and Slaughter (2001) or the German Marshall Fund (2006, question 3.2) for another recent survey showing virtually similar views toward international trade among Americans of different age groups.

and India[25] may start eroding support for international trade among this group.

Third, and of most direct interest to this analysis, America will feel the full impact of the 30-year stagnation in skill levels in the US workforce when many baby boomers begin retiring, which makes expeditious reform of US high-skilled immigration policies imperative. Urgent reforms of the broader US education system[26]—even if immediately and successfully implemented—will produce more young American graduates only in the long term. However, in the short term—say at least over the next decade—only high-skilled immigration can provide American employers with the skilled workforce they need to continue to compete and expand in a global skills-biased economy.

Size and Educational Characteristics of Foreign-Born Populations in Rich Countries

The broader US debate on immigration is occasionally framed within the perception of "American exceptionalism" (Lipset 1996)—that America is the number one destination of immigrants in the world and that US borders are far more open to immigrants than almost anywhere else in the world. This perception is partly rooted in US history—that America was a "New World immigrant nation." Numerically, the United States does take in far more immigrants than any other country today, but it is important to distinguish between simple "immigration size effects"—the United States welcomes more immigrants than other countries because it is a bigger country and has a larger population—and "large-scale immigration." While the United States continues to welcome many immigrants today, it probably welcomes fewer immigrants relative to other rich countries than many Americans believe. This section provides recent comparative data for the OECD countries to illuminate this issue.

One must first carefully and coherently define "immigrants" across different countries. This superficially simple task is severely inhibited by axiomatic dissimilarities in the way different countries organize their

---

25. It is clear that economic liberalization in both India and China in recent decades has brought millions of new highly skilled workers into the global labor force. This, however, is a one-off stock effect almost exclusively the result of trade policy liberalizations and not directly related to longer-term improvements in the average skill levels of the Chinese or Indian populations. Moreover, it can be seen in figure 1.3 that both countries are rapidly expanding the number of university graduates each produces, albeit from a very low base. It is less clear that many of these graduates are all truly available to the global economy. See, for instance, McKinsey Global Institute (2005) for estimates that perhaps only as few as 10 percent of Chinese graduates are truly part of the global workforce.

26. See NCEE (2007) or OECD (2007b) for a list of required reforms.

population censuses. Some define immigrants as foreign nationals—i.e., current residents with foreign citizenship. Given the very large differences among OECD countries in access to citizenship—for instance, it has been traditionally relatively easy to acquire citizenship in most Anglo-Saxon countries while extremely difficult, if not outright impossible, in "blood-line oriented" countries like Germany or Japan—such methodological issues may completely invalidate cross-country comparative data.[27]

Instead, one can use the concept of "foreign-born" from the OECD's Database on Foreign-born and Expatriates[28]—i.e., a resident person born outside the country in question—as a possible intuitively valid definition of "an immigrant."[29] The "foreign-born" definition eliminates any differences in countries' rules for granting citizenship, and valid cross-country data may thus be presented. The "foreign-born" definition, however, ignores cultural or ethnic differences among people born in a given country. The OECD database further relies exclusively on national census data and therefore to the degree that these data are included in the database, it also covers estimates for illegal immigration. Illegal immigrants are thus included in the "foreign-born" data for the United States.

Figure 1.4 shows that while the share of foreign-born in the US population was relatively high in 2005, it was by no means among the highest in the OECD. Other traditional Anglo-Saxon destination countries like Canada and New Zealand, for instance, had shares of foreign-born population fully 50 percent higher than that of the United States, while Australia's was almost double that of the United States. Alpine countries such as Switzerland and Austria also had a higher foreign-born population share than the United States.[30] It is thus erroneous to assume that US borders have been much more open than many other countries or that in relative numeric terms the United States is more of a destination country than many other countries.

The fact that the foreign-born population shares in several continental European countries like Germany, Sweden, Belgium, the Netherlands, and Greece are more than 10 percent—quite similar to, if slightly below, the US level—further underlines the fact that the levels in the United States are far from unusual and certainly not exceptional.

---

27. See Dumont and Lemaitre (2005) for details.

28. The database covers all aged 15 and above. It is available at www.oecd.org.

29. For US data, foreign-born is defined as anyone who is not a US citizen at birth. They include naturalized US citizens, lawful permanent residents (immigrants), temporary migrants (such as students), humanitarian migrants (such as refugees), and persons illegally present in the United States. The latter—illegals—is an important inclusion in US data. See the Census Bureau's website at www.census.gov.

30. See also Lowell (2007) for immigration data for the 1975–2005 period, which show a significant rise in immigrant populations across the developed world.

Figure 1.4   Foreign-born population as share of total population, 2005 or latest available

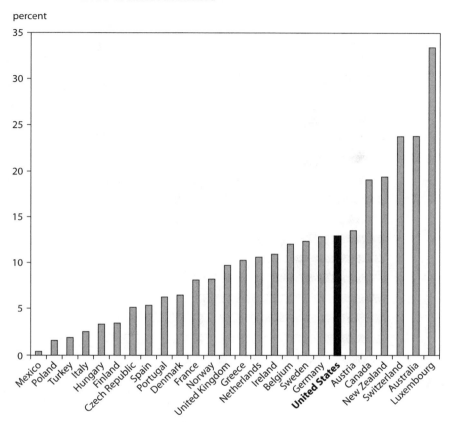

percent

Source: OECD (2007c).

In addition, some commentary on US immigration is rooted in the belief that the immigrant population here is disproportionately low skilled. The most recent data on the educational attainment of foreign-born populations in the OECD are presented in figure 1.5.[31]

The figure illustrates several points: The first bar shows the educational attainment of the entire US population 15 years and older in 2006

---

31. All foreign-born whose educational attainment could be ascertained are included. In some countries, though not the United States, some foreign-born were coded as "unknown" in the OECD database. Generally, the "unknowns" represented a small share (less than 20 percent) of the total number of foreign-born. As there is no immediate reason to believe that the "unknowns" category is systematically biased toward any particular educational category, its exclusion from the data in table A.1 will not impact the conclusions drawn.

Figure 1.5 Educational attainment of foreign-born population, 15 years and above, circa 2000

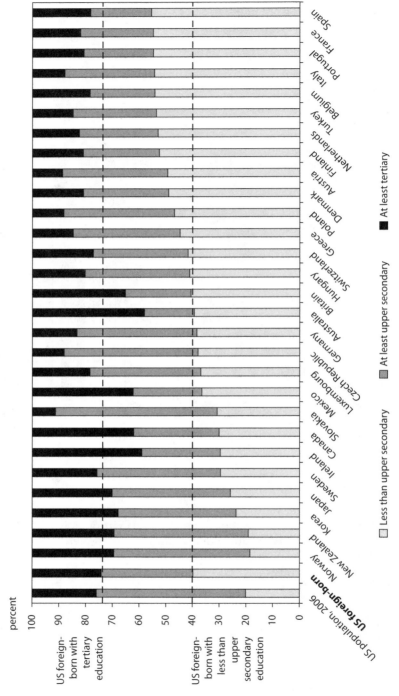

percent

Sources: Bureau of Labor Statistics and Census Bureau, Current Population Survey, available at www.bls.gov/cps; OECD Foreign-born and Expatriates Database.

from the same data source in figure 1.1. The second bar shows the latest available data on the educational attainment of the US foreign-born population. The foreign-born population has slightly more high-skilled people (those with tertiary education) than does the entire US population. By this metric, therefore, the immigrant population is as skilled as the US population at large and decisively not low-skilled relative to the total US population.

However, figure 1.5 shows that the share of foreign-born population with less than secondary education is twice as large (40 percent) as that for the US population as a whole (20 percent). This difference may sound quite dramatic. However, recall that the demarcating feature between having attained at least upper secondary education and not having done so is whether an individual has graduated from high school or not. What figure 1.5 ultimately translates into is that, if one more out of every ten immigrants who have come to the United States had graduated from high school, the foreign-born population would in terms of educational attainment essentially have mirrored the US population as a whole.[32] This difference is definitely not trivial, but it hardly constitutes a flood of relatively low-skilled workers either. Indeed, figure 1.5 seems to validate descriptions of the US immigrant population as being "hourglass shaped" with many high-skilled and many low-skilled individuals.[33]

Equally important, figure 1.5 shows that the overall educational attainment of the US foreign-born population circa 2000 was far from unusual. Several countries have far larger shares of high-skilled foreign-born residents than the United States. The same is true for shares of low-skilled immigrants: A majority of European countries have significantly higher shares of foreign-born residents with less than upper secondary education than does the United States.

The bottom line: The United States is certainly big in immigration terms, but there are few traces of exceptionalism.

High-Skilled Workers in Science and Engineering

A frequently voiced concern about the economic future of the United States is the declining interest among younger Americans in the "hard sci-

---

32. Note further that the relative similarity between the foreign-born population and the US population as a whole enhances the validity of the "time-series use" of the Census Bureau data in figure 1.1. It seems unlikely that any of the particular age cohorts will have been systematically affected in a biased manner by inflows of immigrants.

33. Passell (2007) shows that a higher share of legal immigrants in the United States had at least a college degree than did the US native population in 2005. Smith (2006) shows that the disparity in the number of school years completed between foreign-born aged 25+ and all native-born aged 25+ declined from 2.1 years in 1940 to just 1.3 years in 2002.

ences" of science and engineering (S&E) and the subsequent acute shortage of workers in these fields. It is beyond the scope of this policy analysis to explore this concern in depth,[34] but figure 1.6 on total number of US graduates and share of S&E graduates illustrates a few key points.

First, the relative stagnation in US education since the late 1970s can also be noticed in figure 1.6. While the total number of US graduates at all levels may have continued to rise every year, only up until the mid-1970s did it rise sufficiently fast to also increase as a share of the rising total US population.[35] Figure 1.6 shows that the relative interest in S&E—measured as a share of total graduates at the undergraduate, graduate, and doctoral levels—has hardly declined since at least the mid-1970s. As such, the issue is rather a decline in interest in general educational improvement, as opposed to a relative decline in interest in S&E.

Some might say that these S&E numbers are relatively stable only because today—unlike in earlier decades—many S&E students at America's universities are foreigners rather than American citizens. This is definitely true but not as true as many think when one looks at recent data.

Figure 1.7 shows that the share of foreign graduate S&E students on temporary visas—i.e., neither US-born nor permanent residents—has increased substantially in the last 25 years, even though a recent 9/11-related decline can clearly be identified.[36] However, it is noteworthy that this gradual 25-year increase came from an already relatively high level as early as 1980.[37] At no point since at least 1980 has the foreign share of total engineering graduate students in the United States been below 40 percent. The same has been true for mathematical, physical, and computer sciences since the mid-1980s. In other words, the heavy reliance on foreign S&E students is not a novelty at US universities but has been the state of affairs for at least a generation.

---

34. See, however, National Science Foundation, Science and Engineering Indicators 2006, available at www.nsf.gov.

35. This excludes the four effects from footnote 6, namely immigration, lifelong learning, demographics, and mortality.

36. The effects of 9/11 arise from several issues: tightened US visa requirements, the perception among foreign students that "getting a US visa is hopeless" and their subsequent pursuit of graduate education elsewhere, and aggressive marketing by other destination countries positioning themselves as post-9/11 alternatives to the United States for prospective graduate students from third countries. Note, however, that more recent data from the Institute for International Education (2006) for total foreign student intake by US universities show a rebound in 2005–06.

37. Data from the Institute for International Education (2006, table on International Students by Academic Level, Selected Years 1954/55–2005/06) covering the period from the mid-1950s for the total number of foreign students among US bachelor's, master's, and doctoral students indicate that their numbers swelled dramatically during the 1970s from earlier relatively low levels.

Figure 1.6   Annual number of degrees awarded at US universities and S&E share of degrees, 1966–2004

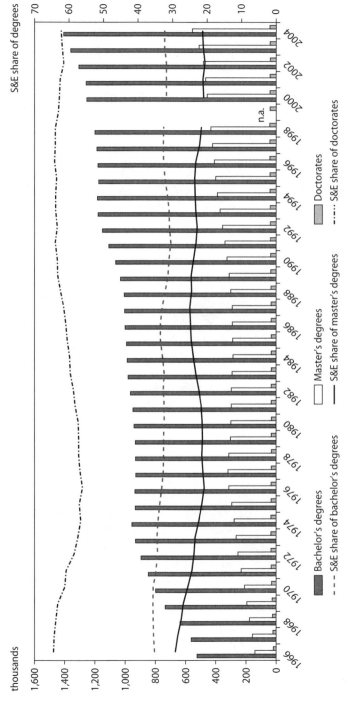

S&E = science and engineering

Note: Data for bachelor's and master's degree holders not available (n.a.) for 1999.

Source: National Science Foundation (2007).

Figure 1.7   Foreign science and engineering students at US universities, 1980–2005

percent share of full-time graduate students
on temporary visas

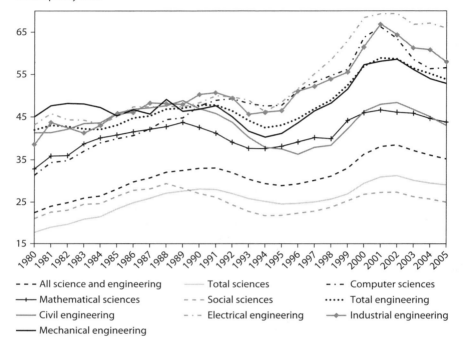

- - - All science and engineering ——— Total sciences - · - Computer sciences
—+— Mathematical sciences - - - Social sciences ····· Total engineering
——— Civil engineering - · - Electrical engineering —♦— Industrial engineering
——— Mechanical engineering

Source: National Science Foundation (2007).

The real issue at present is therefore not that more foreigners are studying S&E in America (they clearly are) but whether or not the United States can maintain its traditionally very high retention rate among highly skilled foreign S&E students. A significant number of these students have historically remained and taken jobs in America upon graduation instead of returning to their countries of origin. Slightly old data from the National Science Foundation (1998) indicate that from 1988 to 1996, approximately two-thirds of foreign S&E doctoral recipients planned to stay in the United States, with the share rising to 79 percent for Indians and 86 percent for Chinese recipients.[38] On the other hand, only 36 percent

---

38. Slightly more recent data in Finn (2005) show that 61 percent of all foreign S&E doctoral

of Korean and 48 percent of Taiwanese recipients intended to stay. As citizens from these four Asian countries accounted for almost 80 percent of all foreign recipients, their intentions mattered. It is noteworthy that the US retention rate among Asian recipients from the more developed economies of South Korea and Taiwan was significantly lower than for China and India. This raises the issue of whether, as China and India gradually achieve developed-economy status and other countries accelerate their intake of Chinese and Indian immigrants,[39] the United States will be able to continue to hold on to the vast majority of S&E graduate students from these two countries or whether Chinese and Indian students will become as likely as South Koreans and Taiwanese to return, as economic opportunities in their home countries and elsewhere improve.

More recent, but less geographically detailed, data from Auriol (2007) indicate that in 2003, fully 40 percent of all recent foreign doctoral degree recipients in the United States intended to leave, indicating that the US labor market may not be quite as attractive as it was in earlier decades. Should this trend of departing foreign graduate and doctoral S&E students accelerate, it would pose a substantial threat to the supply of S&E skills to the US workforce.[40] (See box 1.1.)

At the same time, however, Auriol (2007) also shows that recent doctoral degree recipients who are US citizens are very immobile compared with their noncitizen counterparts, with only 5 percent intending to leave the United States. This indicates that the United States does not suffer any significant hemorrhage of domestic doctoral students and that expeditiously granting foreign students US citizenship could be an effective way of keeping them in the United States after graduation (see also chapter 3).

The age profile of the exiting S&E workforce further accentuates the need to continue to retain a very high level of foreign students in the US workforce. Figure 1.8 shows that, while the age profile of the degree-holding S&E workforce is perhaps slightly younger than the overall university-educated US workforce,[41] a substantial number of S&E degree holders

---

degree recipients in 1998 worked in the United States five years after graduation—i.e., in 2003.

39. Data from OECD (2007c, figure I.8) show that the 2005 share of inflows of Chinese and Indians to all OECD countries with available data (including the United States), except Spain, Italy, Hungary, and the Czech Republic, were significantly above the share of Chinese and Indians in the countries' total stock of foreign immigrants, indicating a relative acceleration in intake from these two countries.

40. This threat is highlighted by the American Electronics Association (2005, 2007).

41. This is not surprising, because computer sciences as a field of study, for instance, has existed in scale only for about 25 years; it hardly existed when the 55–59 year olds entered the workforce.

**Box 1.1   The high-skilled immigrant entrepreneur—shut out
             at America's increasing peril**

The entrepreneurial zeal of many immigrants in America is well known and can be witnessed when walking on the streets of any American city today: A number of restaurants, grocery shops, convenience stores, or dry cleaning businesses are very likely to have been started by recently arrived immigrants. Undoubtedly, this constant inflow of entrepreneurial zeal—and the possibilities to utilize it in a lightly regulated economy—represents one of the biggest economic advantages America has over other countries in the 21st century. This advantage is also captured in the 2006 Kauffman Index of Entrepreneurial Activity, which shows that the incidence of entrepreneurship among immigrants as a whole was on average 25 percent above that of native-born Americans in the decade from 1996 to 2005.[1]

Immigrants are also increasingly becoming a very important component of America's treasured high-tech entrepreneurs. A survey by Duke University and University of California–Berkeley (2007) shows that fully one-quarter of all newly founded engineering and technology firms in America between 1995 and 2005 had at least one foreign-born founder, while in the Silicon Valley area, this share rose to more than half (52 percent). In software, computer/communications technology, and semiconductors, the shares of foreign founders were all over one-quarter the national US average. By 2006, these US engineering and technology companies, fully or partly founded by immigrants in 1995–2005, employed a total of 450,000 Americans and had annual sales of $52 billion.

Another survey carried out by the National Venture Capital Association (2007) of all publicly traded venture capital–backed companies founded since 1970—the vast majority of which can be assumed to have been founded by high-skilled individuals—showed similar results. The survey found a substantial rise in the share of immigrant-founded venture capital–backed companies in America. The share rose from just 7 percent in 1970–80 to 20 percent in 1980–89. This corresponds closely with the finding in this chapter that starting as early as 1980, a large share of science and engineering (S&E) graduate students at US universities were foreign nationals. The share of immigrant-founded venture capital–backed publicly traded companies in America rose to 25 percent between 1990 and 2005. In other words, as all immigrant-founded venture capital–backed companies have been in "S&E type" sectors,[2] it is clear that the large and increasing share of foreign S&E students in America is being directly reflected in America's population of high-skilled entrepreneurs.

Certainly, some successful high-tech firms will be founded by Bill Gates–like college dropouts[3] or others with irrepressible new ideas, but the overwhelming majority of them have been and will continue to be founded by highly skilled people with

(box continues next page)

university degrees in S&E fields. If America wishes to benefit from new eBays, Yahoo!s, or Googles[4] in the future, it must not only maintain its flexible business startup–friendly economy but also ensure that tomorrow's high-skilled technology entrepreneurs gain access into the country in the first place.

1. This index measures the percent of individuals (aged 20–64) who do not own a business in the first survey month but start a business the following month, working 15 or more hours per week (Kauffman Foundation 2006).

2. The sectors involved were high-tech manufacturing; information technology; life sciences; professional, scientific, and technical services; other services; other manufacturing; finance and insurance; and e-commerce (National Venture Capital Association 2007).

3. Incidentally, Harvard University still considers Bill Gates a member of its Class of 1977, despite the fact that he himself claims to have left Cambridge of his own volition in 1975 before graduating. See *FT Observer*, June 5, 2007.

4. eBay's cofounder Pierre Omidyar is French, Yahoo!'s cofounder Jerry Yang is from Taiwan, and Google's cofounder Sergey Brin was born in Russia.

will nonetheless in the coming decade pass into some form of retirement.[42] Moreover, as is the case with the degree-holding US population, younger cohorts aged 30–34 with S&E degrees are not substantially more numerous than their colleagues 20 years older. Unequivocally, therefore, America will (continue to) become ever more reliant on retaining US-trained foreign high-skilled S&E talent in the workforce, both because their share of supply is rising and because the existing stock will increasingly be retiring.

It is beyond the scope of this policy analysis to discuss required reforms of the broader US S&E education system,[43] but the data in this section raise at least two S&E immigration-related issues: US high-skilled im-

---

42. Figure 1.8 shows that more than 300,000 individuals aged 65+ remained in the US labor force in 2003. However, as pointed out in chapter 3 of the National Science Foundation, Science and Engineering (NSF S&E) Indicators 2006, exact retirement age is a complex matter, with part-time jobs frequently replacing previous full-time employment. Table 3.16 in NSF S&E Indicators 2006 shows that by age 62, more than half of all S&E bachelor's and master's degree holders had retired from all types of employment in 2003, while half of the doctoral degree recipients had retired by age 65. The same publication's annex table 3.14 shows that by age 65, just 31 percent of S&E bachelor's and master's degree holders worked full time, while 53 percent of the PhDs did so. This figure corresponds to a total US labor force participation for the 60–64 year olds in 2003 of 51 percent (and rising), 27 percent for 65–69 (and rising), 15 percent for the 70–74, and 6 percent for the 75+ group (Current Population Survey data). Hence the effective retirement age of the US S&E workforce is not that different from the US workforce as a whole.

43. See, however, National Academy of Sciences (2007) for an excellent blueprint on these much-needed reforms.

Figure 1.8   Individuals in US labor force with S&E or S&E-related highest degrees, 2003

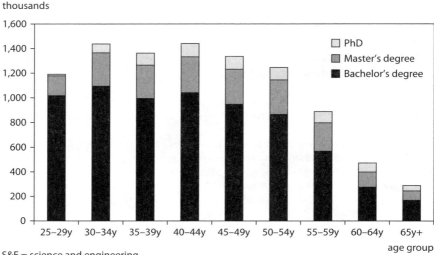

thousands

S&E = science and engineering

Source: National Science Foundation, Science and Technology Indicators, 2006, table 3.13.

migration policies must increasingly focus on retaining US-trained S&E talent in the US workforce and must also remain generally open for continued inflows of foreign-trained S&E workers.

Global High-Skilled Talent: An Increasingly Sought After Resource

International migration can be roughly split into six groups: (1) family-related (through reunions and marriages), (2) humanitarian (typically refugees from United Nations quotas or asylum seekers), (3) employment-related (permanent), (4) employment-related (temporary), (5) student, and (6) illegal. The categories of family-related, humanitarian, and illegal immigrants are of limited interest here, as their high-skilled component is usually limited.[44] The student category is almost exclusively by definition

---

44. As a clear trend exists for the highly skilled to marry highly skilled, there is a possible high-skilled component here, but for the purposes of this analysis, it can be ignored. Passell (2007, table 2) presents data showing that 17 percent of unauthorized immigrants, or 1.3 million, in the United States in 2005 had achieved at least a bachelor's degree. Many in this group likely are individuals admitted on a high-skilled temporary visa like the H-1B or F-1 student visa who have remained in the United States after their visa expiration. This is a significant number, but many of these unauthorized but high-skilled immigrants

made up of high-skilled immigrants, while both permanent and temporary employment migration have high- and low-skilled components. As can be seen in figure 1.9 (which, however, does not include data on illegal immigrants), in 2005 US permanent immigration policy was far less oriented toward employment than those of other OECD countries. Only one-tenth of new permanent immigrants in the United States in 2005 arrived directly for employment-related reasons, compared with more than twice that in Canada, three times that in Australia and New Zealand, and more than four times that share in the United Kingdom and several other European countries.

Rather, the overwhelming majority of permanent US immigration is—as explicitly stipulated by US immigration law—family-oriented. Given this overwhelming dominance of family-related immigration in total US immigration numbers, it is striking that the National Science Foundation (2007) finds that of all US immigrants with an S&E education (about 3.4 million) in 2003, only 37 percent arrived for family reasons; the number declines to 27.5 percent for S&E immigrants who arrived after 1994. Moreover, these numbers are skewed by the arrival of immigrants younger than 18 years at the time of first entry who subsequently went on to pursue S&E education in the United States. Among S&E-related immigrants with a master's degree, the share of family-related immigration drops to 30 percent, while among S&E doctoral degree holders, it is merely 16 percent. In other words, despite dominating total US immigration, family is a far less important issue when it comes to attracting S&E-educated foreigners. As other OECD countries increasingly move toward policies of "managed"—i.e., employment-oriented—immigration, this continued focus of US immigration policy on family seems likely to increasingly put the country at a disadvantage relative to other rich countries in attracting high-skilled workers from third countries, because high-skilled workers are less numerous among family-based immigrant groups.

Training foreign high-skilled workers locally is the easiest way to attract them into a country's workforce. Among international students, the United States remains by a substantial margin the largest destination country, although its share of global foreign students dropped from 25.3 percent in 2000 to 21.6 percent in 2004 (Balatova 2007). Other Anglo-Saxon countries have long competed with US universities for foreign students, but today many non-English-speaking countries, particularly in northern Europe, also offer most S&E courses in English—the globally dominant academic language today—to attract more nonnative students.

---

seem unlikely to take up jobs in occupations where they can fully utilize their high-skilled capabilities. As such, they seem far more likely to take up lower-skilled jobs for which they are therefore likely significantly overqualified. Their number notwithstanding, it remains pertinent to not take them into account in this analysis.

Figure 1.9   International permanent migration by category of entry, selected OECD countries, 2005 (percent of total inflows)

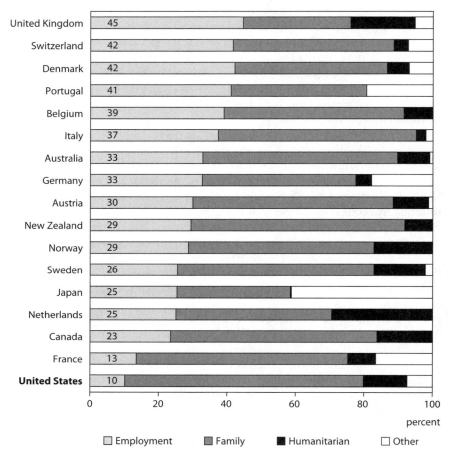

OECD = Organization for Economic Cooperation and Development

Source: OECD (2007c).

Equally important, more countries are now emulating the US policy of offering foreign students an optional one-year work permit upon graduation[45] to entice them to stay. Australia has since 1999 made it relatively easier for foreigners with local degrees to obtain permanent residency via its points-based system, while in 2006 Canada eased the restriction of

---

45. In the United States, this system is known as optional practical training (OPT) and is available once to all foreign graduates from US universities. See, for instance, the page on Applying for F-1 Optional Practical Training at www.oiss.yale.edu for more information.

off-campus work for graduate students and in 2005 made it possible for them to stay for up to two years after graduation.[46] In May 2007 the United Kingdom expanded its year-long optional work visa program for graduates from just S&E fields (since 2004) to cover all bachelor's and graduate degree recipients.[47] In 2007 France introduced its new "first professional experience option," which grants foreign students in degree/diploma tracks the option of a six-month renewable visa to search for and accept employment in France (Murphy 2006). Even the usually highly immigration-resistant German government announced in August 2007 that foreign students who finished their degree in Germany (of which many are in science, technology, and engineering) would be eligible for a three-year work permit upon receiving a job offer.[48] Similar initiatives have also recently been implemented in other EU countries, so the United States as the "market leader" is clearly facing rapidly intensifying competition for foreign students as workforce entrants.[49]

The traditional Anglo-Saxon immigration destination countries of Australia, Canada, New Zealand, and the United Kingdom for a long time have had explicitly skills-oriented immigration policies in place, focusing on granting access to foreigners possessing an adequate number of "skills points."[50] However, as laid out in OECD (2006b and 2007c), and illustrated in figure 1.10, more OECD countries are putting in place immigration systems intended to "actively manage" national immigration, rather than letting it be driven by family-related and humanitarian considerations. Figure 1.10 shows that traditionally other Anglo-Saxon countries have had a higher share of highly educated immigrants than the United States (about 25 percent). In recent years, however, more European countries have surpassed the US share. Even notoriously immigration-resistant Japan in 2006 changed its Immigration Control and Refugee Recognition Act to facilitate immigration of researchers and engineers (OECD 2007c, 98f).

---

46. See Citizenship and Immigration Canada press release, Canada's New Government to Extend Off-Campus Work Program to More International Students, December 14, 2006, available at www.cic.gc.ca; see also the web page on "Studying in Canada: Work Permits for Students" on the same website.

47. See UK Department for Children, Schools and Families, press notice, New International Graduates Scheme—Rammell, March 28, 2007, available at www.dfes.gov.uk.

48. See "Germany Softens Restrictions of Central and Eastern European Workers," Euractiv. com, August 27, 2007, www.euractiv.com.

49. This issue has been explored in greater detail in National Academy of Sciences (2005). Lowell (2007) shows that the inflow of skilled migrants to more developed countries rose rapidly during the 1990s and that European countries increased their share of the increasing total during this period from 20 percent in 1990 to 23 percent in 2000.

50. For a summary description of the Australian high-skilled immigration points system, see White (2007); for Canada, see Clark (2007); and for the United Kingdom, see Feikert (2007). Chapter 3 further discusses these points systems.

**Figure 1.10   Share of immigrant population 15 years and older
with at least tertiary education, circa 2000**

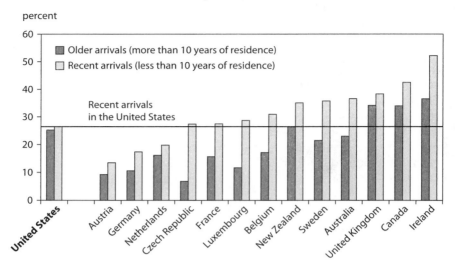

Source: OECD Foreign-born and Expatriates Database.

Managed migration policies invariably mean policies aimed at attracting more high-skilled workers while restricting access to lower-skilled ones. General exceptions are usually made only when it comes to temporary workers in the agricultural sector. The international trend indicating increased competition for high-skilled foreign labor is evident to the degree that similar immigration measures can also be identified among middle-income countries, such as recent EU members and Mexico (OECD 2007c, 96). Indeed, even at the supranational EU level, there are, at the time of this writing, firm signs that change is in the air (and Europe clearly takes inspiration from existing US immigration laws). EU Justice Commissioner Franco Frattini in mid-September 2007 announced that he would shortly propose creating an EU-wide "blue card,"[51] which would provide non-EU skilled workers temporary EU-wide work permits.[52]

Developing countries like China and India, traditionally the two largest sources in numerical terms of high-skilled immigrants,[53] are starting to

---

51. Blue is of course the color of the EU flag.

52. See "EU to Propose Blue Card for Skilled Workers," *EU Observer*, September 14, 2007, http://euobserver.com.

53. High-skilled emigrants from China and India have a share of only a few percent in their domestic high-skilled workforces. Therefore the risk of serious brain drain from these

preempt possible future skill shortages as they themselves experience high economic growth. As a result of recent data that show that only a quarter of the more than 1 million Chinese students who went overseas to study from 1978 to 2006 returned to China (Chinese Academy of Social Sciences 2007), the Chinese government in March 2007 issued new guidelines for "green passage" of acclaimed overseas Chinese scientists, engineers, and executives willing to return to China. This eased passage would include such perks as guaranteed university spots for the children of returnees, exemption from the Chinese household residence registration (*hokou*) and tax preferences.[54] The new policy is aimed at luring back up to 200,000 such overseas Chinese by 2010, which is on top of a 50 percent increase in the number of returnees from 20,000 to 30,000 annually between 2003 and 2005. Should these new Chinese policies prove successful, the United States faces the largest potential adverse impact because it has been the traditional destination of most high-skilled Chinese immigrants.

---

countries is limited. This, however, is not the case for smaller countries particularly in Africa and the Caribbean: Data from the OECD Foreign-born and Expatriates Database show that high-skilled emigrants from these countries make up almost three-quarters of the domestic high-skilled workforce, and hence brain drain concerns are justified.

54. "The Turning Tide of Overseas Chinese," *China Daily*, May 30, 2007; "China Hit by Brain Drain, Report Says," *China Daily*, June 1, 2007.

2

Current US High-Skilled Immigration System

This chapter briefly describes how the present US high-skilled immigration system operates and who the main beneficiaries are. However, it is crucial to first highlight a very important yet frequently ignored technical feature that concerns all data on employment-related visa issuance. When linking any such visa data with labor-market outcomes, it must be kept in mind that visa data are invariably "gross" data. As such, visa data cannot be directly related to developments in the net job data, which include the vast majority of regularly issued official labor-market statistics.[1] Data on employment-related visas can instead be said to most closely resemble gross data on job openings, which are available only from the Bureau of Labor Statistics (BLS) in relative aggregate categories.[2] No corresponding data are available from any source on the number of immigrants who lose their jobs—i.e., visa-related gross job destructions.

The US immigration system distinguishes between permanent and temporary high-skilled immigration.

Permanent High-Skilled Immigration

Every year since 2000 approximately 1 million aliens have obtained legal permanent resident (LPR) status in America.[3] The majority, as mentioned in the previous chapter, are family-sponsored immigrants. But under the

---

1. See Kirkegaard (2005) for an elaborate treatment of this issue.

2. Data from the Bureau of Labor Statistics, Business Employment Dynamics Program, available at www.bls.gov/bdm/home.htm.

3. See Department of Homeland Security data at www.dhs.gov.

Immigration and Nationality Act of 1990, a total of 140,000 employment-based immigrant visas can be allocated each fiscal year—from October 1 to September 30—for workers and their spouses and children.[4] Compared with the annual 65,000 congressional cap on H-1B visas, for instance, this number is quite large, but it is not immediately clear how many of these 140,000 are workers and how many are dependents (spouses or children only). Further, not all of the 140,000 eligible for an employment-based immigrant visa are high-skilled because needed unskilled workers may also qualify.

More important, however, from the perspective of measuring the inflow through this channel of foreign high-skilled workers to the United States, one must distinguish between "new arrivals" who got their employment-based green card (LPR status) abroad and individuals going through an "adjustment of status"—i.e., changing from a temporary (non-immigrant) visa status to LPR status—while already inside the United States. The "adjustment of status" channel does not necessarily imply that a new high-skilled worker has been added to the US workforce but rather that one who is already part of the workforce here or perhaps a graduating foreign student is allowed to remain permanently. About two-thirds of the total of about 1 million new individuals in LPR status each year go through an adjustment in status. But as can be seen in figure 2.1, the share of high-skilled employment-based immigrants who adjust their status here has been significantly higher at about 80 percent over the last decade and rose to more than 90 percent in 2005 and 2006. This trend is most pronounced among those in the highest-skilled E-1 and E-2 categories.

While the extraordinarily large number of adjustments in status in recent years has been linked to temporary changes in US immigration laws,[5] it is nonetheless evident that the green card system, rather than being a major channel for bringing new high-skilled workers to the United States,

---

4. These 140,000 visas are split into five categories: E-1, E-2, E-3, E-4, and E-5. Different rules concerning labor certification, occupations, and skills govern each category. For more information, see the Department of State website at http://travel.state.gov. For the purposes of this policy analysis, only E-1 (priority workers), E-2 (professionals holding advanced degrees or persons of exceptional ability), and E-3 (skilled workers, professionals with a bachelor's degree, and unskilled workers) will be considered high-skilled. The E-3 (the largest) category also includes unskilled workers, hence the data total presented here for skilled workers has an upward bias.

5. The American Competitiveness in the 21st Century Act of 2000 allowed for 130,137 unused employment-based visas from 1999 and 2000 to be made available to E-1, E-2, and E-3 preference employment-based immigrants. Approximately 94,000 of these were used in 2005. The Real ID Act of 2005 further allowed for the recapture of 50,000 unused employment-based visas from 2001 to 2004; 5,125 of these were used in 2005 and 33,341 in 2006. Note also that the annual 140,000 limit may be topped up with any unused family-sponsored visas in the previous fiscal year. As a result, the 140,000 limit is hardly set in stone. See Office of Immigration Statistics (2006, 2007).

Figure 2.1 High-skilled employment-based legal permanent resident flow, FY1997–FY2006

number of workers

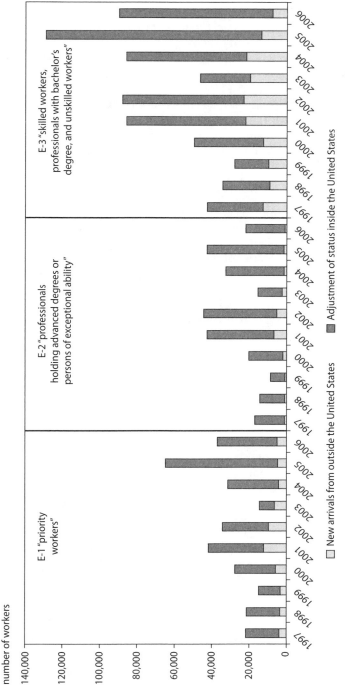

Note: "New arrivals to the United States" equals number of employment-based immigrant visas issued at overseas US consular offices. Data include workers, spouses, and dependents.

Sources: US Department of State, Bureau of Consular Affairs, Reports of the Visa Office, various years; US Department of Homeland Security, Yearbooks of Immigration Statistics, various years.

functions overwhelmingly as a mechanism to ensure that those already legally employed in other visa categories remain in the US workforce. As such, with employment-based green card holders making up only a small part of new foreign entrants to the US workforce, the high-skilled green card program is intricately linked to the primary gateway through which high-skilled workers enter the United States, namely the temporary high-skilled work visa programs (see next section). If reform of either the high-skilled green card program or the high-skilled temporary visa programs is to succeed, then policymakers must acknowledge their symbiotic link. Reform of US high-skilled immigration should, therefore, encompass both permanent and temporary immigration.

The overwhelming use of the LPR system for adjustment of status gives rise to an additional major constraint for individuals already inside the United States. Section 202 of the Immigration and Nationality Act stipulates that the per-country limit for all family and employment-based immigrant visas is 7.1 percent of the annual total, or 25,620.[6] This per-country numerical limit is the reason why citizens of some countries (notably India and China) face oversubscribed categories and hence a very lengthy application process.

Two agencies are involved in the immigrant visa process: the Department of Homeland Security's US Citizenship and Immigration Service (USCIS),[7] which processes visa applications, and the Department of State, which issues the visas and is responsible for maintaining the limits (i.e., keeping track of the number of visas issued). The State Department publishes its count and visa availability each month in its *Visa Bulletin*, which is released two weeks before the first of every month. The USCIS defines the process for issuing green cards and follows the monthly *Visa Bulletins* in determining when to accept applications for adjustment of status.

Eligible foreign nationals in the United States can adjust their status to LPR—in other words, submit their "final" green card applications—when their priority or cut-off date (i.e., place in line) is current according to the *Visa Bulletin*. These dates vary among employment categories and nationalities. For instance, in June 2007 cut-off dates were current for all but four countries, China, India, Mexico, and the Philippines. These dates in June 2007 for E-2 applicants from China and India were January 2006 and April 2004, respectively, while for E-3 applicants the date was June 2003 for both countries as well as Mexico and June 2005 for the Philippines.[8] This means that for Indian E-2 applicants, for instance, only those applications filed

---

6. The limit for dependents is 2 percent, or 7,320.

7. On March 1, 2003, functions of the US Immigration and Naturalization Service (INS) transitioned to the USCIS.

8. No cut-off date existed for E-1 priority workers in June 2007. See Department of State, *Visa Bulletin for June 2007*, available at http://travel.state.gov.

more than three years ago would in June 2007 start being processed in the current fiscal year.

The huge pent-up demand for LPR status among high-skilled workers already inside and employed in the United States is amply illustrated by the administrative upheaval that rattled this system in July and August 2007. In its initial *Visa Bulletin for July 2007* (issued on June 12, 2007), the Department of State announced that all employment-based green card categories, except the third "other workers" category, would be current in July 2007 and removed the hitherto implemented cut-off dates for Indian, Chinese, Mexican, and Filipino high-skilled workers. This decision allowed eligible applicants in all employment categories, regardless of nationality and cut-off dates, to apply for adjustment of status in July.[9]

The State Department made this announcement because it saw many unused visa numbers as the end of FY2007 (September 30) rapidly approached. In past years, many State Department–allocated visa numbers were never used and thus lost because the USCIS, plagued by administrative delays, did not manage to process enough applications to fully use the annual quota. Not wishing to "waste" large numbers of visas this year, the State department intended to front-load visa numbers to allow a large number of applicants to file for adjustment.[10]

This announcement from the State Department evidently "surprised" the USCIS. Realizing that it would not be able to act on so many applications in such a short span of time, it announced a series of changes to the application process and suspended services such as premium processing of immigrant visa petitions (form I-140).[11] Through these tactics, the agency hoped to slow the submission of applications in July.

However, two weeks later, on July 2, 2007—the day the new State Department announcement would have gone into effect—the department reversed its decision, announcing that visa numbers for all employment categories, regardless of nationality, would be unavailable until October 1, 2007, start of the next fiscal year. The department cited the sudden back-

---

9. See Department of State, *Visa Bulletin for July 2007*, available at http://travel.state.gov.

10. See section E in the *Visa Bulletin for July 2007*, Department of State, available at http://travel.state.gov.

11. See USCIS Update: USCIS Announces Temporary Suspension of Premium Processing Service for Form I-140, Immigrant Petition for Alien Worker, available at www.uscis.gov. Premium processing allows petitioners, attorneys, or other representatives to pay an extra $1,000 fee and be assured of a completed process within 15 calendar days; see "How Do I Use the Premium Processing Service?" USCIS, www.uscis.gov. Given the importance of this decision for the petitioners involved, it should be evident that this fee has clear similarities to a traditional "system greasing" bribe, usually paid to government officials in corrupt countries. As such, the premium processing system is not unlike the US political campaign contribution rules in putting an official, institutional, legal façade to what elsewhere is condemned as corruption.

log reduction efforts of the USCIS as the reason behind the reversal of the decision. The USCIS had apparently used up almost 60,000 employ-ment-based visa numbers in June, thus exhausting all numbers available to these categories under the FY2007 annual numerical limit. The same day the USCIS announced that it was "rejecting applications to adjust sta-tus filed by aliens whose priority dates are not current under the revised *July Visa Bulletin*."[12] This announcement left sponsoring US employers and applicants wondering whose dates were current in July and what would happen to rejected applications.

Following a public outcry[13] and a rebuke from the chairwoman of the House Immigration Subcommittee,[14] in mid-July 2007, the USCIS and the Department of State reversed themselves again and announced that the initial *Visa Bulletin of July 2007* would hold, thus allowing all eligible applicants, regardless of nationality and cut-off dates, to file their adjust-ment of status applications no later than August 17, 2007.[15] According to its preliminary estimates, the USCIS had—during the one-month "win-dow of opportunity" for eligible applicants—received more than 300,000 applications for LPR status from high-skilled workers. Compare this with an average of just above 50,000 applications per month earlier in 2007. Evi-dently, plenty of high-skilled foreign workers already employed in the United States wish to stay permanently.

The cut-off dates for Chinese, Indian, and Filipino high-skilled work-ers were reimposed on August 17, 2007. So those who missed the "win-dow of opportunity" will now have to wait for years to even submit their final applications. And those who did submit will have to wait for several months or even years to receive the green card because of the high volume of applications the USCIS received in July–August 2007. Such long, fluctu-ating, and arbitrary wait times will invariably force high-skilled workers already employed in the United States as well as graduating students to leave the country as they graduate from universities or as their tempo-rary work permits run out. In other words, current bottlenecks in the LPR system may push US-trained graduates or already employed high-skilled workers, especially from the countries mentioned above, out of the US workforce.

---

12. See Department of State, Update on July Visa Availability (revised *July Visa Bulletin*), available at http://travel.state.gov; and USCIS Update: USCIS Announces Update on Em-ployment-Based Adjustment of Status Processing, available at www.uscis.gov.

13. See Moira Herbst, "The Gandhi Protests Pay Off," *BusinessWeek*, July 17, 2007.

14. See "US Agency Is Swamped by Requests for Visas," *New York Times*, August 18, 2007 and the website of Congresswoman Zoe Lofgren at http://lofgren.house.gov.

15. See USCIS Update: USCIS Announces Revised Processing Procedures for Adjustment of Status Applications, available at www.uscis.gov.

Temporary High-Skilled Immigration

The United States offers two main temporary visas for employment: L-1 for intracompany transferees (in managerial, executive, or specialty knowledge positions)[16] and H-1B, which is an employer-sponsored visa for "specialty occupation" workers.[17]

L-1 Visa Program

Few data are available on a regular basis from official sources on the L-1 visa category and on the characteristics of the foreign nationals entering the US workforce on such visas. Figure 2.2 shows the issuance of L-1 visas at US consular offices between fiscal years 1996 and 2006. While it is technically possible to adjust visa status into L-1 while inside the United States in a manner similar to the LPR system described above, the transfer requirement of the L-1 visa makes it likely that the numbers in figure 2.2 for L-1 issuance outside the United States will include the overwhelming majority of L-1 recipients inside the United States.

No numerical quotas exist for L-1 visas, and their issuance—assuming unchanged acceptance criteria over time[18]—should therefore broadly reflect the desire of multinational companies to transfer relevant high-skilled employees to the United States. Given the ongoing global integration of the US economy, it is not surprising that the overall issuance of L-1 visas has been rising in the last decade (figure 2.2). It is noteworthy though that Indian nationals have accounted for essentially the entire increase in L-1 visa issuance since 2000, while issuance to citizens of the rest of the world has remained flat. Given that L-1 issuance to Chinese nationals has hardly budged between 1996 and 2006, this increase in issuance to Indian nationals can scarcely be attributed solely to the ongoing global integration of

---

16. The L-1 visa category applies to intracompany transferees who, within the three preceding years, have been employed abroad continuously for one year and who will be employed by a branch, parent, affiliate, or subsidiary of that same employer in the United States in a managerial, executive, or specialized knowledge capacity. It is valid for up to 7 years (5 years for specialized knowledge capacity). No labor certification is necessary. See classifications of temporary workers at http://travel.state.gov.

17. The H-1B visa category applies to persons in a specialty occupation that requires the theoretical and practical application of a body of highly specialized knowledge requiring completion of a specific course of higher education, generally the equivalent of a bachelor's degree. This visa classification requires a labor attestation issued by the Department of Labor.

18. The legal criteria for the L-1 visa category have not changed substantially over the period shown in figure 2.2. However, a number of changes concerning worksite practices and outsourcing were enacted as a result of new rules attached to the Omnibus Appropriations Act of FY2005. See USCIS press release, USCIS Implements L-1 Visa Reform Act of 2004, June 23, 2005, at www.uscis.gov.

Figure 2.2   Issuance of L-1 visas at US consular offices, FY1996–FY2006

number of visas

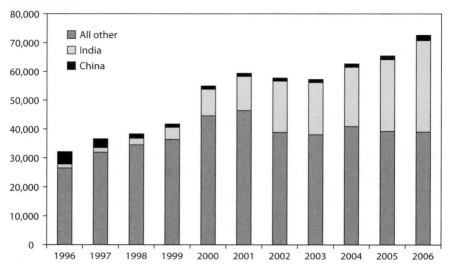

Source: US Department of State, Bureau of Consular Affairs (2000 to 2006).

the Indian economy.[19] It is therefore clear that two simultaneous trends in L-1 visa issuance have existed in recent years: rapid increases concerning Indian nationals and stability concerning citizens of the rest of the world.

In June 2007 the offices of US Senators Richard J. Durbin and Charles Grassley published a specially requested USCIS list of companies that used the L-1 visa in fiscal years 2005 and 2006.[20] The full list for 2006 consists of approximately 18,000 companies, the top 25 of which are listed in table 2.1.

Considering the dearth of and obvious public interest in precise official data concerning the use of US high-skilled visa programs, particularly L-1 and H-1B (see below), it is both remarkable and extremely unfortunate that a special bipartisan request by two US senators is required for such highly relevant data to be made public. Certainly, the public debate over

---

19. This must be the conclusion, even when one allows for the fact that India's economic expansion beyond its borders has been led to a far larger degree by private-sector companies and foreign acquisitions (especially in Europe, with companies like Mittal Steel Company and Tata Steel taking over Arcelor and Corus, respectively).

20. See Office of US Senator Charles Grassley press release, Grassley and Durbin Release New Information on L Visas: List of Companies Using the L Visa, June 26, 2007, available at http://grassley.senate.gov.

Table 2.1   Top 25 L-1 employers, FY2006

Rank	Company	Sector	Home country	Number of visas
1	Tata Consulting Systems	IT services/software	India	5,408
2	Cognizant Technology Solutions	IT services/software	India	1,888
3	Wipro Ltd.	IT services/software	India	1,187
4	IBM	IT services/software	United States	614
5	Hewlett-Packard	IT hardware	United States	417
6	Satyam Computer Services	IT services/software	India	336
7	Intel Corporation	Semiconductors	United States	314
8	Caritor, Inc.	IT services/software	United States	280
9	Ernst & Young	Business services	United States	249
10	HCL Technologies	IT services/software	India	244
11	Infosys Technologies, Inc.	IT services/software	India	235
12	Patni Computer Systems, Inc.	IT services/software	India	221
13	Schlumberger	Oil services	France	198
14	Syntel	IT services/software	United States	197
15	M&E Group, Inc.	n.a.	n.a.	194
16	Exxon-Mobil	Oil	United States	187
17	Kanbay, Inc.	IT services/software	India	178
18	Halliburton	Oil services	United States	157
19	PriceWaterhouse Coopers	Business services	United States	152
20	Oracle, Inc.	IT hardware	United States	148
21	Nokia	Mobile telephony	Finland	141
22	Microsoft	IT services/software	United States	133
23	Perot Systems	IT services/software	United States	121
24	Deloitte	Business services	United States	112
25	HSBC	Financial services	United Kingdom	103

(table continues next page)

high-skilled immigration in the United States would benefit tremendously from such illuminating data if they were published regularly by relevant US immigration authorities. There seem to be no plausible reasons for authorities to not regularly publish such high-skilled immigration data.

Table 2.1 shows that in FY2006, the top 25 users of the L-1 visa program overwhelmingly were Indian information technology (IT) services and software companies, which accounted for approximately three-quarters

Table 2.1 Top 25 L-1 employers, FY2006 *(continued)*

Grouping	Share (percent)	Number of visas
Total top 25		13,414
Total for ~18,000 companies on list		~49,200
Top 25 share of total	27	
India top 25	72	9,697
US/other top 25	28	3,717
IT services top 25	82	11,042
Other sectors top 25	18	2,372
Share of total companies with five or fewer L-1 visa petitions	~95	

n.a. = not available

Note: The source of the data in this table is a comprehensive list of companies using the L-1 visa program in FY2006. The list contains numerous misspellings and multiple entries for different legal entities that are part of the same company. Hence the precise numbers attached to each company must be viewed with caution. This data uncertainty, however, is too small to affect the conclusions drawn from these data.

Source: Office of US Senator Charles Grassley press release, Grassley and Durbin Release New Information on L Visas: List of Companies Using the L Visa, June 26, 2007, available at http://grassley.senate.gov; author's calculations.

of the filings among this group and about 20 percent of the total number of L-1 petitions. Indeed, it can be seen in table 2.1 that the Indian companies are concentrated at the very top, occupying seven of the top 12 spots, while being absent from the lower half of table 2.1. Also, Indian companies have a negligible presence among the rest of the approximately 18,000 companies that in FY2006 used the L-1 program, 95 percent of which requested only five or fewer L-1 visas per company. Due to the different data sources in question, it is not possible to positively conclude that L-1 visas requested by Indian IT services companies go to Indians. Yet, it is nonetheless overwhelmingly likely that the small number of Indian IT services companies listed in table 2.1 account for the vast majority of the rise in overall Indian use of the L-1 visa program (figure 2.2).

While no long time-series data are available for company use of the L-1 visa program,[21] the dual trend in this program indicates rising use of such visas by a limited number of intense users from the Indian IT services industry and stable and diverse use among a very large group of multinational companies from different economic sectors.

---

21. The data published by Senators Grassley's and Durbin's offices do, however, show very similar levels for the top L-1 users in fiscal years 2005 and 2006.

H-1B Visa Program

Available data on the H-1B program, especially on visa issuance and characteristics of recipients, are relatively more detailed than those available for L-1 visas. Table 2.2 shows select data for the last six years, with more detail available in table A.2 in the statistical appendix. Box 2.1 estimates the potential number of H-1B visa holders inside the United States at a given point in time.

Table 2.2 shows data on the characteristics of successful petitions for H-1B visas granted by the USCIS from fiscal years 2000 to 2005 (latest available). The H-1B visa is initially valid for three years, with a three-year extension available. The data are therefore split into two categories: initial employment (first three-year period) and continuing employment (second three-year period). This section focuses on petitions granted for initial employment.

Several things are clear in table 2.2: First it is immediately clear that the number of actual H-1B petitions granted by the USCIS and the congressional cap on H-1B visas of 65,000 are almost wholly unrelated. The total number of H-1B petitions granted not only is much higher than the congressional cap but also actually rose by more than 70,000 from FY2003 to FY2004, despite the fact that the cap was reduced from 195,000 in FY2003 to 65,000 in FY2004. The reason for this seeming discrepancy is not visa fraud on a massive scale, but rather the large number of H-1B petitions that by congressional decision is exempt from being counted toward the cap of 65,000. These exceptions include all petitions granted for continuing employment, as well as all petitions granted to employers in the educational, nonprofit, research, and medical sectors (see below). Any notion that the congressional cap does, or was ever intended by the US Congress to, function as a serious regulatory instrument for the number of H-1B visas granted to foreign workers must therefore be dismissed.

Second, the total number of H-1B petitions granted fluctuates quite significantly from year to year. After peaking in FY2001, the total number dropped by about 40 percent—about 135,000—in FY2002 and was fairly flat through FY2003 before rising substantially (and even exceeding the congressional cap) by more than 70,000 in FY2004. Unsurprisingly, the majority of this fluctuation is found among petitions granted for initial employment, but some of the FY2004 spike was due to the rise in petitions for continuing employment (up more than 40,000 from FY2003)—a "three-year echo" of the more than 200,000 petitions granted for initial employment during the peak year of FY2001.

As in the LPR system, a distinction should be made between H-1B petitions granted to individuals outside the United States at the time of filing and individuals inside the United States at the time of the employer filing on their behalf. The latter would be a functional equivalent to adjustment

Table 2.2   H-1B petitions granted by the USCIS, initial and continuing employment, by selected characteristics, FY2000–FY2005

Line	Characteristic	FY2000
	H-1B cap legislated by Congress	115,000
1	Total number of H-1B petitions granted by USCIS	257,640
2	Of which: number of H-1B petitions granted, for initial employment	136,787
3	Of which: aliens were outside the United States at the time of employer petition	75,785
4	Of which: aliens were inside the United States at the time of employer petition	61,002
5	Of which: were from India	60,757
5a	Of which: were not from India	76,030
6	Of which: were from China	12,333
7	Of which: started working in computer-related occupations	74,551
7a	Of which: did not start working in computer-related occupations	62,236
8	Of which: started working in IT services industry	n.a.
8a	Of which: did not start working in IT services industry	n.a.
9	Of which: number of H-1B petitions granted for continuing employment	120,853
10	Of which: were from India	63,940
11	Of which: were from China	10,237
12	Of which: continued employment in computer-related occupations	73,875
13	Of which: continued employment in IT services industry	n.a.
14	Fiscal year average unemployment rate for US workers aged 16 and above (percent)[b]	4.0
15	Fiscal year average unemployment rate for computer programmers (percent)[b]	2.3

n.a. = not available

USCIS = US Citizenship and Immigration Service

a. Includes 20,000 H-1Bs for foreign graduates from US universities.

b. Estimated as the average of Q4 (previous year) and Q3 (current year) from Bureau of Labor Statistics and Census Bureau, Current Population Survey (CPS) release (16 years and above) and quarterly data on employed and experienced unemployed persons by detailed occupation and class of worker, table 3 from the CPS (computer programmers).

Note: The shaded areas in the table denote H-1B petitions that are exempt from the congressional cap on H-1B visas.

FY2001	FY2002	FY2003	FY2004	FY2005	Change, FY2001– FY2002	Change, FY2003– FY2004
195,000	195,000	195,000	65,000	85,000[a]		
331,206	197,537	217,340	287,418	267,131	−133,669	70,078
201,787	103,584	105,314	130,497	116,927	−98,203	25,183
115,759	36,494	41,895	60,271	54,635	−79,265	18,376
85,320	67,090	63,419	70,226	62,292	−18,230	6,807
90,668	21,066	29,269	60,062	57,349	−69,602	30,793
111,119	82,518	76,045	70,435	59,578	−28,601	−5,610
16,847	11,832	11,144	11,365	10,643	−5,015	221
110,713	25,637	28,879	56,559	52,353	−85,076	27,680
91,074	77,947	76,435	73,938	64,574	−13,127	−2,497
88,613	17,803	19,347	47,362	44,644	−70,810	28,015
113,174	85,781	85,967	83,135	72,283	−27,393	−2,832
130,127	93,953	112,026	156,921	149,932	−36,174	44,895
70,893	43,914	49,897	63,505	61,171	−26,979	13,608
10,483	7,009	8,919	14,893	13,918	−3,474	5,974
80,684	49,477	54,235	70,720	61,515	−31,207	16,485
60,071	35,814	39,323	51,182	43,550	−24,257	11,859
4.3	5.7	6.0	5.6	5.2	+ 1.4	− 0.4
2.7	6.3	6.8	6.0	2.6	+ 3.6	− 0.8

Sources: US Department of State, Bureau of Consular Affairs (2000 to 2006); INS (2000b, 2002a, 2002b); US Department of Homeland Security, Office of Immigration Statistics (2003b, 2004b); USCIS (2006a, 2006b). It must be emphasized that the USCIS caveats these reports on H-1B visas by stating that "very little editing has been done to the data," and there may consequently be some errors in the data. Whether these errors are likely to be systematic cannot be discerned.

Box 2.1   How many H-1B visa holders are there in the United States?

Estimating the number of H-1B visa recipients inside the United States at any given point in time is fraught with difficulty, as gross data are available only for the number of visa petitions granted and actual visas issued. Any estimate will therefore have to rely on assumptions concerning the departure date of the visa holder. The intuitively most sound approach seems to be to assume that an H-1B visa holder remains employed within the United States for the entire duration of the visa.

Assuming, therefore, that H-1B visa holders remain in the United States for the full three years their visa is valid and drawing on the data in table 2.2 and appendix table A. 2, one is presented with several options for estimating a total potential number of H-1B visa holders inside the United States. It is important to note that such estimates represent an upper-bound estimate. These are presented in table 2.B1.

Table 2.B1   Total potential number of H-1B visa holders in the United States, 2001–05

Category	2001	2002	2003	2004	2005
Total potential H-1B petitions approved	n.a.	786,383	746,083	702,295	771,889
Total potential H-1B visas issued	411,446	413,285	387,191	364,513	370,261
Total potential Indian H-1B visa holders	n.a.	351,238	305,707	267,713	321,253
Total potential H-1B visas issued to Indians	190,670	179,620	160,335	149,994	159,561
Total potential H-1B visa holders in computer-related occupations	n.a.	414,897	349,625	285,507	324,261

n.a. = not available

Sources: Table 2.2 and appendix table A.2.

If one looks first at the total number of H-1B petitions, one can see that about 750,000 foreign high-skilled workers could potentially have been legally present in the United States on H-1B status between 2002 and 2005, assuming that all approved petitions were used and everyone stayed for the entire three-year period. This upper-bound estimate equals about 1.4 to 1.5 percent of the total US high-skilled population with at least a bachelor's degree over this period.[1]

At the same time, however, row 2 shows that only about half as many were issued H-1B visas and could have been present from 2001 to 2005. This number excludes all

(box continues next page)

aliens who changed their visa status to H-1B while already inside the United States and therefore is significantly lower than the actual total at any given time. As such, the true number of H-1B visas holders inside the United States lies in the range of numbers in rows 1 and 2,[2] or between 370,000 and 770,000 in 2005.

A similar estimation yields a number for potential Indian H-1B holders of between 160,000 and 320,000 in 2005 (rows 3 and 4). A potential 324,000 H-1B visa holders in computer-related occupations could have been present in the United States in 2005, which was 90,000 fewer than in 2002 but 40,000 more than in 2004 (row 5). No data exist for the number of H-1B visas actually issued to aliens in computer-related occupations, and no lower-bound estimate is therefore available for this category.

---

1. In 2005 there were 54.7 million US residents with at least a bachelor's degree (US Census Bureau at www.census.gov).

2. More sophisticated estimates can be made, for instance, by adjusting the population numbers for deaths, projected levels of emigration from the United States (i.e., early returns), and transfers to permanent US residence. See Lowell (2000). However, introducing such additional assumptions in the estimations is both beyond the scope of this policy analysis and unlikely to materially affect the results.

in status in the LPR system. All H-1B petitions granted for continuing employment must fall in this latter category, as do a little more than half of the petitions for initial employment (line 4 in table 2.2).[22] INS (2000b) data indicate that the majority of individuals for whom a petition for initial employment is filed while inside the United States are students adjusting their status from F-1 student visa to H-1B temporary worker. Given that the one-year optional practical training (OPT) period of legal employment is available to all F-1 students graduating from US universities for a minimal fee compared with the costs of an employer filing for an H-1B visa,[23] it seems reasonable to assume that many students transferring to H-1B status do so while already employed in the United States on OPT and as such do not contribute to new inflows of high-skilled workers to the US economy. However, it is certain that this group of foreign students trans-

---

22. The share of petitions filed for people inside the United States was about 45 percent in 2001 and rose to 65 percent in 2002 before declining to between 50 and 55 percent in 2004–05.

23. In order for a student to enter the 12-month OPT period, he/she must pay only a $180 fee for the employment authorization form I-765 submitted to the USCIS, compared with employer costs of up to $5,000 for filing an application for H-1B status, as reported in Anderson (2006).

ferring to H-1B status constitutes a substantial part of the retention of foreign science and engineering (S&E) students highlighted in the previous chapter. Hence it is comforting to note that this group is relatively stable in size at about 60,000 to 70,000 and does not seem to have particularly suffered after 2001.

Moreover, while the annual extra quota of 20,000 H-1B visas made available in May 2005 to foreign graduates with a US master's or higher degree was not exhausted during the remaining five months of FY2005,[24] the entire quota of 20,000 visas for FY2006 was exhausted within less than four months into the fiscal year in January 2006.[25] The quotas in fiscal years 2007 and 2008 have also been fully used (see below).

By far the most sensitive segment of H-1B issuance is the number of petitions granted for initial employment to individuals outside the United States (line 3 in table 2.2)—in other words, to the segment that introduces new high-skilled workers to the US workforce. It declined by more than 70 percent from FY2001 to FY2002, accounting for more than 80 percent of the total decline that year, while rising more than 40 percent from FY2003 to FY2004, accounting for just under three-quarters of the total rise.

Cross-tabulations of data from different rows in table 2.2 are not available. But data on petitions for initial employment for the top two countries of origin (lines 5 and 6), top occupation (line 7), and top industry (line 8) reveal that, as in the L-1 program, Indian nationals dominate the H-1B program and that most recipients work in computer-related occupations and/or in the IT services industry. Besides, it is clear that a large part of the decline of about 80,000 from FY2001 to FY2002 in initial employment petitions originating from outside the United States is found in all three groups, namely Indian nationals, computer-related occupations, and IT services sector (second column from right). The same is true for the rise in petitions for initial employment during FY2003–FY2004 (far right column). These data thus suggest that one group of workers, namely Indians who are granted initial employment in computer-related occupations in the IT services industry while outside the United States at the time of the petition filing—a group of obvious interest in the offshoring debate—is the most irregular group of all H-1B recipients. While they make up approximately half of all petitions for initial employment, they also account for the vast majority of the fluctuation in the total number of H-1B petitions granted for initial employment.

---

24. The USCIS announced at the end of June 2005 that it had received only 8,069 petitions. See USCIS press release, USCIS Announces Update Regarding New H-1B Exemptions, June 12, 2005, available at www.uscis.gov.

25. See USCIS press release, USCIS Reaches H-1B Exemption Cap for Fiscal Year 2006, January 18, 2006, available at www.uscis.gov.

At the same time, table 2.2 indicates that use of the H-1B system by employers on behalf of individuals who account for roughly the other half of petitions for initial employment (captured in lines 5a, 7a, and 8a)—i.e., those who are not Indian, not employed in computer-related occupations, or do not work in the IT services sector—is relatively stable at approximately 70,000 to 80,000 petitions per year, excluding the peak year of FY2001.

Similar to the dual trend in L-1 visas, two distinct India-related trends can be identified in the H-1B program: volatility concerning inflow of new (for initial employment) high-skilled workers from India and relative stability concerning the inflow of such workers from the non-India world. Moreover, additional data for the H-1B program indicate that the former trend is concentrated among workers in computer-related occupations and in the IT services sector.

While one should generally avoid comparing gross visa data with labor-market outcomes, it is nonetheless clear from lines 14 and 15 of table 2.2 that the volatile half of H-1B petitions for initial employment tended in both 2001–02 and 2003–04 to behave as one would theoretically expect "data on gross job openings" to behave—i.e., the number of petitions for initial employment fell drastically when US unemployment rose in 2001–02 and rose when US unemployment fell in 2003–04.[26] This movement is particularly pronounced when one compares the H-1B initial employment data with the unemployment rate for a key group of workers in the offshoring debate—computer programmers (see below). This group experienced a very large rise in unemployment during 2001–02, which exceeded the unemployment rate for the total economy, but in 2005 returned to essentially full employment at between just 2 and 3 percent unemployment, a level at which it has remained until the last available data for 2007Q2.

At the same time, table 2.2 clearly shows that even as the US unemployment rate among computer programmers was rising in FY2001–02, more than 25,000 new H-1B recipients entered the US workforce in computer-related occupations during that period. As no data are available for the number of foreigners on H-1B visas who exited computer-related occupations in this period, the net employment and wage impact of these movements in this occupational category cannot be immediately discerned (see chapter 3).

Data from the USCIS on the number of H-1B visa petitions granted to individual firms are not available on a regular basis.[27] Data for the

---

26. In some respect it mirrored the experience of the total number of gross private job openings in the US economy, which peaked in 2000Q4 and started to rebound only in 2003Q4. In 2001Q2 US gross job losses for the first time since 1992 exceeded the number of gross job openings. Data from the Bureau of Labor Statistics, available at www.bls.gov/bdm/home.htm.

27. Firm-level data on H-1B foreign labor certification applications are available at the De-

1999–2000 period are available from INS (2000a), and Senators Durbin and Grassley published in June 2007 a special release of the top 200 companies in terms of H-1B recipients in 2006 based on USCIS data.[28] Table 2.3 shows the top 25 companies on the senators' list (full list is supplied as table A.3 in the statistical appendix)[29] and their home countries and business sectors.

The top 25 account for 35,829 H-1B visas granted in 2006, just below half of the total 77,851 for the top 200[30] (data are not yet available for the entire H-1B program for 2006). Indian IT services/software companies clearly dominate the top of the ranking, occupying 7 spots out the top 10 and 13 of the top 25 and accounting for fully two-thirds of the H-1B visas granted in the top 25 (almost 24,000), while US firms in IT services/software, education, financial services, and other sectors account for the remaining third (about 12,000 H-1B visas). These firm-level data thus corroborate the finding in table 2.2 of a substantial group of H-1B recipients from India working in computer-related occupations and the IT services sector. The lack of firm-level time-series data prevents an affirmative analysis of whether the use of the H-1B program by the top Indian IT services firms fluctuates as much as indicated in table 2.2 or whether the fluctuation in table 2.2 is accounted for by other companies recruiting Indian nationals.

Again, however, it must be emphasized that these firm-level data are of a "gross job creation" nature and do not necessarily indicate, for instance, that number one ranked Infosys increased its foreign high-skilled workforce in the United States on H-1B visas by almost 5,000 in 2006 alone. Instead, based on data from the company's filings with the Securities and Exchange Commission (SEC), table 2.4 shows that the number of H-1B visa holders in Infosys in 2006 was up by a still substantial 1,780, when accounting also for foreign workers whose visas expired and who thus subsequently exited this visa status and presumably left the United States. It should, however, be emphasized that the extensive use of a "project-based on-site delivery" model by companies like Infosys, where individual

---

partment of Labor FLC database at www.flcdatacenter.com. These data capturing "an interest in applying," however, are very different from the actual number of H-1B petitions granted by USCIS and hence should not be used to analyze visa quantities or the number of actual new foreign high-skilled immigrants entering the US labor market.

28. See Office of US Senator Charles Grassley press release, Grassley and Durbin Release New Information on L Visas, June 26, 2007, available at http://grassley.senate.gov.

29. The full list of 200 companies is from *InformationWeek*, May 17, 2007, based on data obtained by this news organization from the offices of the senators in question.

30. It is not clear from the statements from the offices of Senators Durbin and Grassley whether the data in table 2.3 equal all H-1B petitions granted to each company or only those for initial employment. The assumption here will be that these data incorporate all H-1B petitions granted.

Table 2.3   Top 25 H-1B employers, 2006

Rank	Company	Sector	Home country	Number of visas
1	Infosys Technologies, Ltd.	IT services/software	India	4,908
2	Wipro Ltd.	IT services/software	India	4,002
3	Microsoft Corporation	IT services/software	United States	3,117
4	Tata Consultancy Services Ltd.	IT services/software	India	3,046
5	Satyam Computer Services Ltd.	IT services/software	India	2,880
6	Cognizant Tech Solutions Corporation	IT services/software	India	2,226
7	Patni Computer Systems, Inc.	IT services/software	India	1,391
8	IBM Corporation	IT services/software	United States	1,130
9	Oracle, Inc.	IT services/software	United States	1,022
10	Larsen & Toubro Infotech Ltd.	IT services/software	India	947
11	HCL America, Inc.	IT services/software	India	910
12	Deloitte & Touche LLP	Accounting	United States	890
13	Cisco Systems, Inc.	ICT hardware	United States	828
14	Intel Corporation	Semiconductors	United States	828
15	I-Flex Solutions, Inc.	IT services/software	India	817
16	Ernst & Young LLP	Accounting	United States	774
17	Tech Mahindra Americas, Inc.	IT services/software	India	770
18	Motorola, Inc.	ICT hardware	United States	760
19	Mphasis Corporation	IT services/software	India	751
20	Deloitte Consulting LLP	Consulting	United States	665
21	Lancesoft, Inc.	IT services/software	India	645
22	New York City Public Schools	Education	United States	642
23	Accenture LLP	Consulting	United States	637
24	JPMorgan Chase & Co.	Financial services	United States	632
25	Polaris Software Lab India Ltd.	IT services/software	India	611

(table continues next page)

H-1B recipients work on-site with US-based clients for the duration of a given project rather than for the duration of the H-1B visa, makes estimating "true" net employment levels for high-skilled workers highly problematic.

Table 2.3   Top 25 H-1B employers, 2006 *(continued)*

Grouping	Percent share of total visas	Total number of visas
Total top 25		35,829
Total top 200		77,851
Top 25 share of total top 200	46	
Indian top 25	67	23,904
US top 25	33	11,925
IT services/software top 25	81	29,173
Education top 25	2	642
Financial services top 25	2	632
Other sectors top 25	15	5,382
Total top 26–200		42,022
Top 26–200 share of total top 200	54	77,851
Indian top 26–200	3	1,349
US top 26–200	92	38,838
Other countries top 26–200	4	1,835
IT services/software top 26–200	28	11,966
Education top 26–200	37	15,587
Financial services top 26–200	10	4,210
Other sectors top 26–200	24	10,259

ICT = information and communication technology

Source: Marianne Kolbasuk McGee, "Who Gets H-1B Visas? Check Out This List," *Information Week,* May 17, 2007; author's calculations.

It is obvious from the tables in this chapter that a small number of Indian-based IT services companies are indeed very heavy users of the H-1B and L-1 visa programs and that the existence of these high-skilled visa programs is integral to their business in the United States.[31] However, it is also clear from table 2.3 that the use of the H-1B program beyond the top 25 users—i.e., among those ranked 26 to 200—was very different during 2006. This group accounts for 54 percent of the total number of H-1B visas in the top 200 (see bottom of table 2.3). Indian IT services/software companies are largely absent from this group. US educational institutions are the biggest individual sector in this group, accounting for more than

---

31. This fact can be easily verified by looking at the SEC filings of several Indian top 10 companies. Infosys, Wipro, Patni, and Satyam all have 20-F filings available in the EDGAR database on the SEC website, www.sec.gov/edgar. Under the sections concerning risks to forward-looking statements, all these companies list "restrictions on immigration" as a factor that could affect their ability to compete for and service US-based clients, which might hamper companies' growth and adversely affect their revenues.

Table 2.4   Infosys employees on US temporary employment visas, 2003–07

End of company fiscal year	Approximate number of H-1B visa holders	Net change from previous year	Approximate number of L-1 visa holders	Net change from previous year
March 31, 2003	4,090		1,760	
March 31, 2004	3,200	−890	700	−1,060
March 31, 2005	4,350	1,150	700	0
March 31, 2006	6,130	1,780	790	90
March 31, 2007	7,100	970	650	−140

Source: Company Annual 20-F Filings with the Securities and Exchange Commission.

a third (37 percent) of visas granted, with largely non-Indian IT services/software accounting for 28 percent of the visas and financial services and other sectors making up the rest.

The dual India-related nature of the H-1B program found at the aggregate level is thus also explicit at the firm level: A small number of Indian IT services/software companies dominate the program in the top 25, but at the lower tiers, far more numerous US companies in a variety of sectors account for the demand for foreign high-skilled workers. The fact that these two relatively distinct groups of "customers" are using the H-1B high-skilled visa program (likely also the L-1 program) gives rise to a number of policy issues, which will be covered in the next two chapters. It is, however, erroneous to draw policy conclusions concerning the overall use and impact of the H-1B program based exclusively on the characteristics of the most intensive users at the top of table 2.3.

In summary, this chapter illustrated how the green card program for high-skilled workers is overwhelmingly a second step aimed at adjusting the status to permanent residency by already employed high-skilled workers in the United States and that high-skilled Chinese and Indian nationals face significant delays in obtaining their green cards. Second, an India-related dual trend exists in the main temporary high-skilled immigration system comprising the L-1 and H-1B programs: L-1 issuance for Indians is rising rapidly and in 2006 was dominated by a limited number of IT services companies. However, L-1 issuance is stagnant for high-skilled workers from other nationalities and generally spread over a very large number of multinational companies, the vast majority of which requested only fewer than five L-1 visas in FY2006. Detailed data for H-1B issuance show a similar dual trend, with a small number of Indian IT services/software companies among the most intensive users of the H-1B program, ahead of a far more diverse group of US companies.

3

Welfare Trade-Off, US Software Workers, and Immigration Quotas

This chapter first considers the broad efficiency versus equity trade-off related to high-skilled immigration and then takes an in-depth look at the labor-market situation faced by the group of US workers most affected in recent years by foreign high-skilled immigration—software workers. Finally it considers the best ways to match foreign workers with US employers and why the use of quotas in high-skilled immigration policies should be avoided.

Welfare Economic Efficiency Versus Equity Trade-Off

High-skilled immigration sets itself apart from other types of migration by its explicit focus on human capital and skills. Hence it must predominantly be oriented toward generating economic growth by easing high-skilled labor shortages in America in the short term and broadly expanding the productive labor capacity in the long run. At the same time, of course, high-skilled immigration policies ought not to be blind to the rights of American workers and should strive to minimize any adverse economic impact on them. The foreign labor certification (FLC) process in US high-skilled (as well as other) immigration law seeks to achieve this latter goal.

This process is managed by the Department of Labor's Employment and Training Administration (ETA) with the explicit aim of ensuring that "the admission of foreign workers into the United States on a permanent or temporary basis will not adversely affect the job opportunities, wages, and working conditions of U.S. workers" and "certification may be obtained in cases where it can be demonstrated that there are insufficient qualified U.S. workers available and willing to perform the work at wages that meet or exceed the prevailing wage paid for the occupation in the area of intended employment."[1] This policy covers only the applications in employment-based legal permanent resident (LPR) status categories E-2 and E-3 and in the H-1B program. LPR status category E-1 and the L-1 temporary visa do not require an FLC and are instead solely conditional on the applicant meeting the visa category criteria[2] and having a US-located job offer.

Much public discourse concerning particularly the H-1B visa has centered on whether the FLC is credible or not and by extension therefore on whether this process adequately protects US worker rights.[3] It is beyond the scope of this policy analysis to adequately evaluate whether or not this is legally the case with the present FLC system. On the other hand, the international trend in the degree to which other OECD governments use FLC-like "labor-market testing" in relation to high-skilled workers is clear: More OECD countries have been scaling it back in recent years. The OECD's *International Migration Outlook 2007*, in a section illustratively titled "Towards the end of labour market testing," notes that in the OECD countries, it has broadly been the case in recent years that

> [o]n the basis of a precise evaluation of the shortages in certain branches and professions, labour market testing has been lifted for a wider range of occupations. (OECD 2007c, 97)

In other words, other OECD countries are clearly less concerned in today's global economic environment than in previous periods about the welfare impact of high-skilled immigration on their native high-skilled workforces. Ironically, therefore, other OECD countries today are increasingly more "free traders in high-skilled people" than is the "traditional immigrant destination country" of the United States. This observation is pertinent for the efficiency-equity trade-off debate in America.

Chapter 1 established that the compositional improvement of the US labor force will slow dramatically and possibly stop entirely in the next decade as a result of the 30-year stagnation in the skill levels acquired by

---

1. The process is described on the ETA website at www.foreignlaborcert.doleta.gov.

2. The E-1 "priority worker" LPR status requires that the applicant present extensive documentation showing sustained national or international acclaim and recognition in the field of expertise. For the L-1 visa, the sponsoring company must provide proof that the applicant is hired into a US-located managerial, executive, or specialized knowledge capacity.

3. See, for instance, US House of Representatives, Subcommittee on Immigration, Citizenship, Refugees, Border Security, and International Law Oversight Hearing on "Is the Labor Department Doing Enough to Protect U.S. Workers?" June 22, 2006; GAO (2006); Miano (2007); and Hira (2007).

workforce entrants and the imminent retirement of the highly educated baby boomer generation. Meanwhile, other OECD countries continue to rapidly improve their workforce skill levels. Simply put, America in the 21st century is no longer a skill-abundant country relative to an increasing share of the rest of the world. On the efficiency side, this slowdown in US labor force skill improvement implies that for America to regain its historical status as the most skill-abundant country in the global economy, it must—as even successful education reforms will have an impact only in the long term—expand high-skilled immigration in the short to medium term. On the equity side, ironically, it implies that the labor-market situation for US high-skilled workers—i.e., those with at least a four-year college degree—will in all probability remain benign. "Getting a degree" will continue to be the ticket to a financially secure "good life" as plenty of well-paying jobs are and will be available for graduates new and old. This situation is already manifested in the unemployment rate for high-skilled US workers, which in the latest available data in 2005 was 2.3 percent (and falling relative to that for other workers),[4] while their wages were almost 50 percent (and rising again) higher than those of high school graduates.[5] Moreover, as high-skilled immigrants generally function as complements rather than substitutes to the native workforce, the wages of high-skilled Americans—unlike those of low-skilled workers—are typically not adversely affected by the increased labor-market competition from high-skilled immigrants.[6] (See next section on US software workers.)

In the aggregate, therefore, it seems appropriate to ask whether high-skilled American workers as a group possess a strong prima facie case for government protection in the form of strict labor-market testing and numerical limits on the number of high-skilled immigrants that can enter the United States. I clearly believe that they do not. Shielding high-skilled American workers from labor-market competition in today's era of accelerating skill shortages and increased global competition for talent is simply not an appropriate area for much, if any, US government intervention.

---

4. See footnote 22 in chapter 1.

5. See Economic Policy Institute, Datazone, Wage and Compensation Trends, table on estimated wage premium for college and high school graduates, 1973–2005, available at www.epi.org/datazone/06/college_premium.pdf.

6. The degree of substitutability between immigrants and native workers will tend to be higher in lower-skilled jobs with fewer training costs and limited language, professional, institutional, and licensing requirements. Orrenius and Zavodny (2007) find that newly arrived high-skilled immigrants in professional occupations have a positive impact on natives' wages, suggesting likely complementarities between, for instance, recently arrived high-skilled temporary workers on H-1B visas and native workers. Friedberg (2000) shows that the returns to skills for immigrants who have acquired educational and professional experience in their home countries are lower in the United States. See also CEA (2007), Ottaviano and Peri (2006), and Borjas (1999). Borjas (2003), however, finds that wages for college graduates declined 4.9 percent due to high-skilled immigration.

Hence, if existing US high-skilled immigration laws remained unchanged in the years ahead, it would represent a remarkable example of regulatory capture and successful rent-seeking strategic behavior by a high-skilled and otherwise privileged special interest group. The result would be the redistribution of economic rents[7] to this group, but at the expense of overall economic growth prospects of the US economy.

Software Workers: The Most Affected High-Skilled Americans

The economics literature has generally found that high-skilled (unlike low-skilled) immigrants have no adverse effects on native workers.[8] A brief look at the fate of high-skilled software workers will be illustrative, as it will allow for a test of this general hypothesis on a particular group of affected high-skilled workers of obvious policy and media interest. Chapter 2 found that a large number of Indian nationals have been offered jobs in computer-related occupations in the United States in recent years, particularly through the L-1 and H-1B programs. Similarly, a great deal of anecdotal evidence on US software workers losing their jobs to Indians on high-skilled visas has been reported in the US press, as well as presented at hearings before the US Congress.[9] American software workers would thus seem an obvious group of high-skilled Americans adversely affected by high-skilled immigration. Indeed, given that computer-related companies and occupations dominate the L-1 and H-1B high-skilled immigration programs (chapter 2), it is implausible that US workers in any other single occupation could have been adversely affected by high-skilled immigration to the same degree. In other words, if adverse effects on native US high-skilled workers cannot be discerned among US software workers, then such adverse effects would be highly unlikely among US workers in other high-skilled occupations, which have experienced far lower inflows of foreign high-skilled workers.[10]

---

7. The term "economic rents" is used here in its usual Ricardian sense: the difference between what a factor of production is paid and how much it would need to be paid to remain in its current use.

8. See, for instance, CEA (2007), Orrenius and Zavodny (2007), Lowell (2007), Passell (2007), Ottaviano and Peri (2005), Camota (1997), and Friedberg (2001). Borjas (2003) finds that unskilled workers are even more negatively affected by immigrants than are high-skilled workers.

9. See, for instance, testimony by John Miano before the Subcommittee on Immigration, Citizenship, Refugees, Border Security, and International Law on March 30, 2006 and June 22, 2006 or the testimony of David Huber before the same committee on March 30, 2006.

10. This statement is based only on comparing the "quantitative supply" of foreign high-skilled immigrants, which is far higher in software occupations than in others. It is possible

As tentatively alluded to in table 2.2, however—and as elaborated in this section—the actual labor-market devastation that American software workers have experienced in recent years is far from obvious, either in employment or wage terms.

As can be seen in figure 3.1,[11] unemployment rates for computer programmers have historically been significantly below the overall unemployment level in America. However, following the collapse of the internet bubble and the end of the Y2K mania, unemployment rose by mid-2002 to above the level for the total US economy. In late 2004, however, unemployment rates for computer programmers again fell below that of the total economy and have since 2005 been about 2 percent or about the level for all university graduates (2.3 percent in 2005). Allowing for frictional unemployment, levels close to 2 percent imply essentially full employment. As such, the aggregate data show that unemployment among computer programmers in America for the last two years has been negligible. Figure 3.1 shows a similar trend in the other major software occupation, that of software engineers,[12] for whom data are available only for 2000–2007: a sig-

---

that American-born workers in other occupations, with less job creation in recent years (or outright net job losses) than has been observed among software occupations, could be more affected by lower numbers of high-skilled foreign immigrants. However, this seems improbable given the very high numbers for high-skilled software-related immigrants and the diversity among "nonsoftware" high-skilled immigrants.

11. Figure 3.1 combines data from the National Science Foundation for computer programmer unemployment from 1983 to 1999 with more recent unemployment data from the detailed occupational tables in the Current Population Survey by the Bureau of Labor Statistics (BLS) and US Census Bureau, as well as available BLS Occupational Employment Statistics (OES) employment data from 1999 to 2007. The OES website, www.bls.gov/oes, lists several methodological reasons why one should be careful with using OES data as a time-series as is done in figure 3.1. However, the data presented in figure 3.1 are national employment data for all industrial sectors in only the 2000 Standard Occupational Classification and do not concern occupations in which seasonal variation is a major concern. Consequently, the methodological considerations regarding time-series use of OES data are nonmaterial for the data used here. OES data have been published at irregular intervals since 1999, but the survey data values are benchmarked to either May or November reference periods. As such, in the treatment here, OES data will be referred to as either Q2 (May data) or Q4 (November data). For more methodological detail, see technical notes for the May 2006 OES estimates at the BLS website at www.bls.gov/oes/current/oes_tec.htm.

12. This policy analysis has chosen a relatively narrow definition of software workers, including only computer programmers and software engineers. This is an intentional attempt at isolating the experiences of a group of high-skilled workers who have been subject to overwhelming media interest in recent years. Further, it is an intuitively valid demarcation of software workers as the following BLS employment classification descriptions show. The BLS definition of "Computer Programmers" (SOC 15-1021) is: Convert project specifications and statements of problems and procedures to detailed logical flow charts for coding into computer language. Develop and write computer programs to store, locate, and retrieve specific documents, data, and information. May program websites. The BLS definitions of the two "software engineers" categories, "Computer Software Engineers, Applications" (SOC 15-1031) and "Computer Software Engineers, Systems Software" (SOC 15-1032), are as fol-

Figure 3.1 US software employment and unemployment, 1983–2007

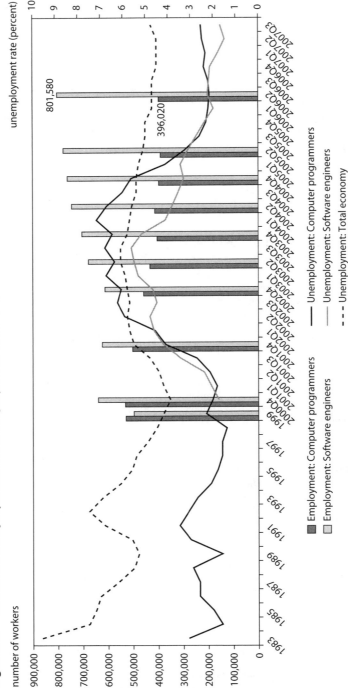

number of workers

unemployment rate (percent)

801,580

396,020

■ Employment: Computer programmers   —— Unemployment: Computer programmers
▢ Employment: Software engineers   —— Unemployment: Software engineers
                                              - - - Unemployment: Total economy

Note: Annual data for 1983–99; four-quarter lagging moving average for 2000–2007; "software engineers" includes both applications and systems software. The availability of data used in this figure has been irregular due to repeated changes by the Bureau of Labor Statistics in the survey methodology.

Sources: National Science Foundation; Bureau of Labor Statistics and Census Bureau, Current Population Survey, available at www.bls.gov/cps; Bureau of Labor Statistics, Occupational Employment Statistics, available at www.bls.gov/oes.

nificant rise after the technology bust, followed by a return to full employment by 2005. While in the constant creative destruction in the dynamic US economy, even high-skilled software workers often lose their jobs (or equally likely leave voluntarily for another) and hence do not have full job security, a 2 to 3 percent unemployment rate indicates that they have near complete employment security (see box 3.1).

Turning to software employment numbers, the bars in figure 3.1 show that at the time of the earliest available data in 1999, there were roughly the same number of computer programmers and software engineers in America, at about half a million each. During the peak year of the internet bubble in 2000, the number of US computer programmers was flat, while the number of software engineers rose by about 125,000 to a combined employment level of about 1.15 million at the peak of the bubble. Following the internet bust, US software employment declined by about 100,000 workers, mostly computer programmers, to about 1.05 million at the trough by end of 2002. During 2003, employment among software engineers rebounded strongly, while that of computer programmers continued to decline to about 400,000 by 2004, a level at which it has since remained roughly steady. Employment of software engineers in 2006Q2 (latest available) had risen to a record more than 800,000, pushing total US software employment to a new record of 1.2 million.

Recall box 2.1, which estimates that the total number of H-1B workers in computer-related occupations in the United States could have been up to 324,000 in 2005. It is important to note here that the category of computer-related occupations is significantly broader than just the two occupations included in software employment (computer programmers and software engineers). Hence, directly relating these two datasets would be akin to comparing apples and oranges. The closest occupational category to computer-related occupations is the broader Standard Occu- pational Classification of SOC 15-0000 "Computer and Mathematical Occupations."[13] In May 2005 total net employment in this category was 2.95 mil-

---

lows: "Computer Software Engineers, Applications"—Develop, create, and modify general computer applications software or specialized utility programs. Analyze user needs and develop software solutions. Design software or customize software for client use with the aim of optimizing operational efficiency. May analyze and design databases within an application area, working individually or coordinating database development as part of a team. Exclude "Computer Hardware Engineers" (SOC 17-2061); "Computer Software Engineers, Systems Software"—Research, design, develop, and test operating systems-level software, compilers, and network distribution software for medical, industrial, military, communications, aerospace, business, scientific, and general computing applications. Set operational specifications and formulate and analyze software requirements. Apply principles and techniques of computer science, engineering, and mathematical analysis. These definitions are available at www.bls.gov/oes.

13. This SOC major group comprises the following occupations: Computer and Information Scientists, Research; Computer Programmers; Computer Software Engineers, Applications; Com-

Box 3.1   The secure US job market for software workers in 2007

Despite much concern, especially during the 2004 US presidential campaign, the US software sector has so far not relocated to India. Rather, it has in recent years positively thrived in global competition, any adverse effects from offshore outsourcing notwithstanding. Moreover, rapidly rising wages for high-skilled Indian workers suggest that the scope for further large-scale offshore outsourcing of US software work solely for the purposes of labor arbitrage may be narrowing. Recent anecdotal data suggest that salaries for top Bangalore-based software engineers have risen from 20 to 75 percent of US levels in just two years from 2005 to 2007,[1] while most wage surveys for broader categories of experienced workers still indicate that Indian wages are at about half of US levels.[2] Evidently, while there are thousands of highly skilled and competent Indians in the country's software sector, they are just not as cheap as they used to be, relative to US workers.

It is encouraging that literally thousands of high-skilled software positions are currently available in the United States. A quick search of US-based directly software-related job openings at the online career center of Microsoft, the largest US software company, at members.microsoft.com/careers, on September 28, 2007 yielded 15 vacant positions for software architect, 716 vacant positions for software development engineer, and 515 vacant positions for software development engineer in testing/software test engineer.[3]

A similar search on the same day at the online career center at IBM at www-03.ibm.com/employment/us for all positions in software engineering requiring a bachelor's, master's, or doctoral degree yielded 1,469 regular full-time US vacancies. Yet another similar online search, also on the same day, at Oracle, another large US software company, at www.oracle.com/corporate/employment/index.html, yielded more than 500 US-based vacant positions in product development posted during the preceding three-month period. In other words, in less than 10 minutes of searching on websites of just three large US software companies, this author found almost 3,000 vacancies for high-skilled software workers located all over the United States.[4]

Thankfully, one of the most vocal opponents of the H-1B visa program, the Programmers Guild, implicitly acknowledges this extremely benign job market for high-skilled US software workers in its April 2007 online newsletter. It states the following in response to a direct inquiry from a Microsoft hiring manager seeking high-skilled US software workers:[5]

(box continues next page)

Box 3.1 The secure US job market for software workers in 2007
(continued)

Microsoft hiring manager seeks your resume

This is not an April Fools' joke. Microsoft has several hundred openings, and a hiring manager has provided his personal email address, asking us to submit our resumes directly to him.

I encourage everyone who has at least a BS degree in Computer Science to send your resume. If American programmers don't even apply for these positions, then it is difficult to argue that we are being displaced by the H-1b workers who do apply. [emphasis in original]

Qualifications? Ideally you will have skills like SQL, C#, .NET or C++, or similar experience and competence in the Microsoft development platform. However, since Microsoft is sponsoring H-1b visas for new graduates—and H-1b workers cannot be hired until October 2007—a BS or higher degree alone should be sufficient for many of the positions that Microsoft is holding open for the H-1b workers it is sponsoring. . . .

With thousands of US-based high-skilled software positions available and a rapidly declining wage differential with Bangalore-based software engineers, the present and future labor market for US software workers in the global economy seem secure. Clearly, some high-skilled US software workers will lose their jobs, and for some it will likely be due to offshore outsourcing. However, with thousands of high-skilled software positions available in the United States, an unemployment rate of 2 to 3 percent, and rising total software employment, this group patently has employment security. Rather than guaranteeing workers their current jobs for life, a dynamic economy should provide them with the chance to always be able to find new jobs.

Some hedge fund managers will lose money even in a rising market, but bailing them out is hardly good government policy. Considering that many less-skilled US workers, for instance, in the manufacturing sector, face genuine hardships—the loss of both job and employment security—as a result of rapid technological innovation and increased global competition, it seems improbable that high-skilled US software workers would have any credible claim for scarce congressional attention or support.

1. "Bangalore Wages Spur 'Reverse Offshoring,'" *Financial Times*, July 1, 2007. See also Hewitt Associates LLC (2006) for wage data showing that double-digit real wage increases for Indian professionals have far outstripped those in other countries in recent years.
2. "Engaging India: Outsourcing in Jeopardy?" *Financial Times*, August 2, 2007. The rising wage trend in India seems to be pushing multinational companies to increasingly sell their captive units in India to local companies, which are better able to achieve economies of scale in operations for multiple clients.
3. These results include all US locations, products, and job subcategories.
4. The author conducted similar searches on the same websites on July 9, 2007 and obtained a similar result of more than 3,000 vacancies in the categories listed.
5. See Programmers Guild E-Newsletter, April 2007, available at www.programmersguild.org.

lion workers. Hence, H-1B visa holders in computer-related occupations potentially present in the United States that year could at the most have amounted to about 11 percent of net employment in computer and mathematical occupations. This share is seven times higher than the share of all H-1B visa holders (roughly 1.5 percent) in the total high-skilled US population.

What about the most important labor-market price signal: wages? What has happened to the wages of US software workers in recent years? In terms of base wages, which exclude benefits, nonproduction bonuses, and supplementaries,[14] computer software engineers, at about $84,000 per year in 2006, earned about 20 percent more on average (25 percent in terms of median wages) than did computer programmers (just below $70,000 on average), reflecting the higher skill content of their work. In the aggregate, US software workers, therefore, earned between two and three times the US median base wage of $30,400 in 2006.[15]

As can be seen in table 3.1a, base wages rose in nominal terms across the wage range by an average 25 to 30 percent from 1999 to 2006 for these groups of workers. This rise was about five percentage points above the rate of inflation over the period. Only the highest-earning computer programmers in the 75th percentile did worse, at about 17 percent base-wage growth over this period. This latter group of software workers therefore had negative base-wage growth from 1999 to 2006, as the consumer price index (CPI) rose by almost 20 percent from 1999Q4 to 2006Q2. Nonetheless, despite this outcome, computer programmers in the 75th percentile earned more than $85,000 before any benefits, bonuses, or supplementaries in 2006.[16] It is not possible to discern from the Bureau of Labor Statistics (BLS) Occupational Employment Statistics (OES) data any trends in the

---

puter Software Engineers, Systems Software; Computer Support Specialists; Computer Systems Analysts; Database Administrators; Network and Computer Systems Administrators; Network Systems and Data Communications Analysts; Computer Specialists, All Other; Actuaries; Mathematicians; Operations Research Analysts; Statisticians; Mathematical Technicians; Mathematical Science Occupations, All Other. See www.bls.gov/oes. Italicized occupational categories are included in "software employment" above.

14. In detail, OES survey wages include straight-time gross pay, exclusive of premium pay. Base-rate cost-of-living allowances, guaranteed pay, hazardous-duty pay, incentive pay including commissions and production bonuses, tips, and on-call pay are included. Back pay, jury duty pay, overtime pay, severance pay, shift differentials, nonproduction bonuses, employer cost for supplementary benefits, and tuition reimbursements are excluded. See OES technical notes at www.bls.gov/oes/current/oes_tec.htm.

15. This number is the annual median wage estimate for "All Occupations" from the May 2006 BLS OES estimates. See table A.4 in the statistical appendix for more details.

16. The BLS OES program covers only full-time and part-time wage and salaried workers in nonfarm industries. The survey does not include self-employed owners and partners in unincorporated businesses, household workers, or unpaid family workers, which means that independent self-employed IT consultants are not included in these data.

Table 3.1a   Annual base wages of US software workers, 1999 and 2006 (US dollars)

Occupation	Mean wage	10th percentile wage	25th percentile wage	Median wage	75th percentile wage	90th percentile wage	Consumer price index
Computer programmers							
1999Q4	54,960	29,650	38,780	51,060	72,780	91,260	168.4
2006Q2	69,500	38,460	49,580	65,510	85,080	106,610	(1999Q4)
Change, 1999Q4–2006Q2 (percent)	26.46	29.71	27.85	28.30	16.90	16.82	
Software engineers							
1999Q4	65,969	40,036	50,179	63,873	80,652	98,142	201.7
2006Q2	84,155	51,086	64,796	82,075	101,286	122,225	(2006Q2)
Change, 1999Q4–2006Q2 (percent)	27.57	27.60	29.13	28.50	25.58	24.54	19.77

Sources: Bureau of Labor Statistics, Occupational Employment Statistics, available at www.bls. gov/oes; Bureau of Labor Statistics, Consumer Price Indexes, www.bls.gov/cpi.

value of non–base wage remuneration for US software workers from 1999 to 2006 and therefore not possible to answer the question whether there are systematic biases in the base-wage to non–base wage remuneration ratio across the wage spectrum. This would be the case, for instance, if the highest-earning software workers received a higher share of their total remuneration in the form of, say, stock options than did workers at the low end of the wage spectrum.

Table 3.1b shows that in terms of relative base-wage growth between 1999 and 2006, US software workers belong to the top quintile of the US workforce when compared with the wage growth in other major occupational categories.[17] US workers in only three major occupational categories—management, healthcare practitioners, and business and financial occupations (in other words bosses, doctors, and bankers), representing 14 percent of the total US wage and salaried workforce—saw higher median wage increases than did US software workers over this period. In the aggregate, not too bad for an occupation that over the 1999–2006 period experienced very large relative inflows of foreign high-skilled workers (see chapter 2). The bottom line: Any detrimental effect on software workers' wages from the inflow of foreign high-skilled workers is far from obvious.[18]

It is important to elaborate on the period chosen for tables 3.1a and 3.1b, because the starting and end points of wage growth estimations similar to those in tables 3.1a and 3.1b are crucial. The 1999–2006 period was chosen first and foremost because complete data are available for that period. It is not possible to go back to a starting year earlier than 1999 because the BLS survey methodology was changed in 1999. At the same time, it is historically evident that software workers went through a tremendous boom-bust cycle from 1999 to 2001–02. The fact that data are available from 1999 onward, however, offers a nice opportunity to slice through the top of the internet boom-bust variation. In 1999Q4 (the period to which the 1999 estimates are benchmarked), total US employment was 130.2 million, while at the end of the March–November 2001 recession in December 2001 it was 130.7 million after having peaked at a seasonally adjusted value of 132.6 million in February 2001. Using 1999 data as the start-

---

17. The level of occupational categories at which one makes this comparison is important, as individual subgroups within the major occupational category shown in tables 3.1a and 3.1b may differ from the higher classification category value. As can be seen in table A.4 in the statistical appendix, the threshold for inclusion in the 90th percentile measured at the level of the total workforce in 2006 was $72,960, indicating that the average computer programmer was about $2,500 away from inclusion in the 90th percentile.

18. Findings in Aldonas, Lawrence, and Slaughter (2007) indicate that as a group in terms of real money earnings (real money earnings in this analysis exclude the value of benefits and equity/stock option grants and are deflated by the CPI), both US college graduates and US master's degree holders saw declines in the period 2000–2005. In other words, US software workers in all probability did far better on wages than even the majority of other US high-skilled workers during this period.

ing point is therefore a sensible approximation of the "sustainable level of employment," thus eliminating the final and worst bubble excesses from 1999 to 2000.

Given the intensity of the boom in software-related occupations in the late 1990s, one would expect this particular category of workers to have experienced the highest wage increases among US workers from 1999 to 2001 while at the same time also a sharper drop during the subsequent bust. Figure 3.2, which shows the real median base-wage developments for US software workers relative to selected occupational categories, illustrates that at least part of these predictions indeed materialized.[19]

Computer programmers (in particular) and software engineers did experience the highest base-wage growth rates of any major occupational category from 1999 to 2001, after which management occupations overtook them. However, it is noteworthy that US software workers "gave up" fewer of these "boom-year" median-wage gains during the subsequent bust than what one would have predicted, especially considering the continued inflow of foreign high-skilled workers to these occupations (see chapter 2). Instead, median wage developments for US software workers after 2001 pretty much mirrored those among other occupational categories—i.e., were basically flat.[20] Hence, by 2006 this group of high-skilled workers was still found to be among the top quintile of American workers in terms of wage growth over the entire 1999–2006 period. As can also be seen in figure 3.2, American workers who have really suffered in terms of relative real wage growth are those in traditional low-skilled occupations, such as food preparation, personal care, and construction.

While the aggregate real base-wage developments for US software workers in recent years have not been as buoyant as these workers would have liked, they are nonetheless on par with the—likely equally disappointing—real wage developments in the broader US economy. As such, there is precious little empirical support for assertions that US software workers have been adversely affected by the large inflows of foreign high-skilled workers to their occupation. Instead, they have held their ground quite nicely in an overall economic environment of stagnant real wages (see table A.4 in the statistical appendix for a detailed listing of employment and real wage developments in US occupations from 1999 to 2006).

This section has perhaps not definitively answered whether US software workers have been adversely affected by foreign high-skilled entrants to the workforce, because it does not address the hypothetical

---

19. The deflator used is the BLS CPI, all items, seasonally adjusted city average. Data for "All Occupations" are available only from 2001 onward.

20. As can be seen in figure 3.2, the biggest beneficiaries of the 1999–2001 internet boom, computer programmers, have from 2001 to 2006 seen a small decline in real wages similar to that found among some lower-skilled occupations.

Table 3.1b Change in base wages for major SOC groups, ranked by median wage change, 1999–2006 (percent)

Occupation	Mean wage	10th percentile wage	25th percentile wage	Median wage
Management	42.0	42	42	40.64
Healthcare practitioners and technical	37.1	30	31	33.45
Business and financial operations	30.2	27	27	28.54
Software engineers	27.6	28	29	28.50
Computer programmers	26.5	30	28	28.30
Life, physical, and social sciences	30.7	26	25	27.43
Computer and mathematical (all)	26.1	21	24	27.20
Architecture and engineering	28.3	24	26	26.76
Protective services	24.9	20	25	24.25
Farming, fishing, and forestry	21.2	18	20	23.96
Sales and related	26.9	18	22	23.52
Healthcare support	24.4	23	24	23.22
Legal	27.8	24	26	22.88
Community and social services	23.3	22	22	22.86
Education, training, and library	25.7	28	24	22.39
Production	20.0	18	20	22.36
Office and administrative support	20.0	17	19	21.24
Arts, design, entertainment, sports, and media	22.5	27	24	21.18
Building and grounds cleaning and maintenance	19.4	17	20	20.70
Transportation and material moving	19.6	18	19	19.23
Installation, maintenance, and repair	19.0	18	19	18.95
Food preparation and serving related	18.1	9	13	18.89
Personal care and services	12.9	12	16	17.21
Construction and extraction	16.8	18	18	15.00

n.a. = not available

SOC = Standard Occupational Classification

Note: Wages from the Bureau of Labor Statistics, Occupational Employment Statistics survey are straight-time, gross pay, exclusive of premium pay. Base rate, cost-of-living allowances, guaranteed pay, hazardous-duty pay, incentive pay including commissions and production bonuses, tips, and on-call pay are included. Excluded are back pay, jury duty pay, overtime pay, severance pay, shift differentials, nonproduction bonuses, employer cost for supplementary benefits, and tuition reimbursements. Shaded occupations are the focus of this chapter.

Sources: Bureau of Labor Statistics, Occupational Employment Statistics, available at www.bls.gov/oes; Bureau of Labor Statistics, Consumer Price Indexes, www.bls.gov/cpi.

75th percentile wage	90th percentile wage	Annual average wage, 2006Q2 (US dollars)	Annual median wage, 2006Q2 (US dollars)	Share of total US employment (percent)	Cumulative share of US employment (percent)
38	n.a.	91,930	80,980	4	4
36	43	62,030	51,980	5	10
31	32	60,000	53,690	4	14
26	25	69,500	65,510		
17	17	84,155	82,075		
33	35	59,660	53,010	1	1
28	26	69,240	66,130	2	3
28	27	66,190	62,390	2	5
25	25	37,040	32,070	2	7
22	21	21,810	17,950	0	8
26	29	34,350	23,160	11	18
25	27	24,610	22,870	3	21
20	n.a.	85,360	67,730	1	22
23	23	39,000	35,790	1	23
24	26	45,320	41,100	6	29
19	18	30,480	27,360	8	37
21	19	30,370	28,080	17	54
19	18	46,110	38,340	1	56
21	19	22,580	20,290	3	59
18	17	29,460	25,300	7	66
19	18	39,060	36,720	4	70
21	24	18,430	16,430	8	79
16	9	22,920	19,070	2	81
15	18	39,290	35,450	5	86

Figure 3.2 Real median wages, selected occupational categories, 1999–2006 (1999Q4 = 100, CPI deflated)

index (1999 = 100)

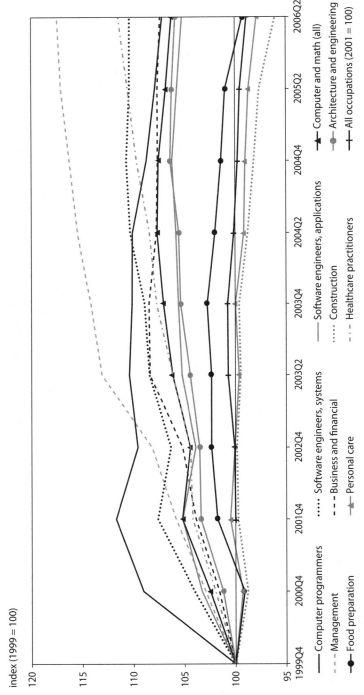

CPI = consumer price index

Source: Bureau of Labor Statistics, Occupational Employment Statistics, available at www.bls.gov/oes; Bureau of Labor Statistics, Consumer Price Indexes, All Items Data, www.bls.gov/cpi.

question of what would have happened to US software workers if foreign high-skilled worker inflows were absent. Such "what if" estimates require substantially more data than what are available for the detailed category of software workers.[21] From the standpoint of basic labor economics, it is straightforward to hypothesize that, in the absence of inflows of foreign high-skilled workers to their occupation from 1999 to 2006 (described in chapter 2), US-based software workers would in all probability have seen even higher wage increases than what were found to have materialized (tables 3.1a and 3.1b and figure 3.2). However, given the findings here—that we are dealing with a group of American workers who in terms of base-wage increases from 1999–2006 belong to the top quintile—the pertinent policy question cannot be, How much more would US software workers have earned without the H-1B visa program, for instance? Instead, a more pressing policy question must be: At what costs to the rest of the US economy would additional economic rents accruing to this group come?

In summary, this section has raised several noteworthy issues concerning the labor-market situation US software workers have faced in recent years.

First, unemployment rates among software workers have been at full employment levels since 2005. Second, employment in software occupations in mid-2006 (latest available) was at an all-time high at 1.2 million workers. Third, the composition of the software workforce has changed, with higher-skilled software engineers making up two-thirds of the total software workforce in 2006 and computer programmers one-third, as opposed to both having been at the same level in 1999. This general development toward higher skill content in the US software workforce is predictable for a high-wage country. Fourth, between 1999 and 2001 base wages of the US software workforce—which are at two to three times the US average base wages—rose faster than those in any major US occupational category, while from 2001 to 2006 they changed at essentially the same rate as those for the rest of the US workforce. Finally, real base wages for the US software workforce have risen substantially more than

---

21. See Borjas (2001, 2003) and Ottaviano and Peri (2006) for examples of such approaches, utilizing factor proportions models and attempts to control for endogenous effects (i.e., that immigrants disproportionately settle in areas with high levels of wage increases). These approaches, however, work on more aggregate worker categories where more data are available. Madeline Zavodny (2003) attempts to estimate the wage and employment impacts of the H-1B program using the number of the Department of Labor's so-called labor condition applications (LCAs)—the first step in an H-1B application—as a proxy. This is an admirable attempt by Zavodny to use available data to shed light on this issue. However, as described in Kirkegaard (2005), the data uncertainties related to the firm-level LCA data (available at www.flcdatacenter.com) are so daunting that their validity is terminally impaired. Zavodny (2003, 7) nonetheless concludes that "H-1B workers also do not appear to depress contemporaneous earnings growth.... H-1Bs do not appear to have an adverse impact on contemporaneous unemployment rates."

base wages earned by more than 80 percent of the total US workforce. This rise in wages has come despite a significantly larger presence of foreign workers on H-1B visas in computer-related occupations than in other high-skilled occupational categories. This clearly suggests that foreign workers in this field are in general complements to US workers, rather than substitutes.

These findings make it hard if not impossible to convincingly argue—media anecdotes notwithstanding—that the aggregate labor-market situation facing the US software workforce has, after a postinternet boom downturn, been or remains anything other than booming relative to the rest of the US economy despite far larger inflows of foreign workers than in any other high-skilled area in recent years. These findings thus follow earlier studies such as Lowell and Christian (2000), the National Research Council (2001), and Zavodny (2003), all of which found that adverse effects of the H-1B program on native US workers could not be estimated with confidence.

These findings thrust a heavy burden of both proof and responsibility onto the shoulders of those publicly espousing the view that young Americans have next to no future in software occupations due to the inflow of foreign high-skilled workers to the United States, as well as the broader phenomenon of offshoring in the IT sectors.[22] It would be a tragedy if young people in the United States today were indeed turned off from pursuing careers in software occupations due to excessive alarmist rhetoric on this subject instead of being given the facts on the actual labor-market situation, based on empirical investigations using official publicly available data, such as those presented in this policy analysis.[23]

Furthermore, recent developments in the United Kingdom are consistent with the finding that high levels of foreign workers have had no significant adverse effects on US software workers. Data from the UK Home Office show that during 2006, 33,756 new work permits were issued to foreign IT workers. About 80 percent (26,835) were issued to Indian IT workers. As the total UK workforce was only about one-fifth of that in the

---

22. For an example of such a line of argument, see, for instance, Hira and Hira (2005), in particular the foreword in it by Lou Dobbs.

23. It is noteworthy that this concern is not an isolated US phenomenon. In their September 2007 communication to the EU Council concerning the imminent shortage of e-skills in the European Union, the European Commission notes: "Higher-level e-skills cannot be easily encoded, which puts a premium on these skills in a European workforce context. The issue is debated in the media as the emergence of a significant restructuring of the labour market. Several sources report a deterioration of the image of the ICT sector and ICT work, which is reflected in the decline in the number of students starting ICT courses" (European Commission 2007, 5).

United States in 2006,[24] this figure would correspond to an annual inflow of foreign IT workers to the United States in 2006 of more than 170,000 (of which about 140,000 would be Indians). This number is a third more than the peak inflow to the United States in 2001, when about 110,000 H-1B visas for initial employment in computer-related occupations were issued (see table 2.2). Simultaneously, in 2006, wages for IT professionals in the United Kingdom rose by substantially above the national UK average to £34,500 (about $65,000 in 2006).[25] The UK data further illustrate that large inflows of foreign, especially Indian, technology workers are not limited to the United States and that other countries are increasingly permitting such inflows.[26]

US law sensibly requires that the foreign high-skilled entrants to the workforce requiring an FLC be paid the "prevailing wage," which is defined by the Department of Labor "as the average wage paid to similarly employed workers in the requested occupation in the area of intended employment."[27] It is beyond the scope of this policy analysis to evaluate whether computer-related or other foreign high-skilled H-1B workers are generally remunerated according to US law.[28] Opinions vary significantly on this matter,[29] but as laid out earlier, the overall labor-market situation facing US software workers is quite auspicious. Given the very high concentration of H-1B use among a limited number of IT services and software companies, any enforcement effort to ensure that US laws are being adhered to in this sector would seem quite manageable, especially as each H-1B (and L-1) application must (since May 2005) be accompanied by a special $500 "fraud prevention and detection fee," which is earmarked for enforcement.[30]

It is noteworthy that in June 2007 the Department of Labor settled a major case for $2.4 million (or about $4,000 per person) with Patni Computer Systems, Inc.—one of the top 10 H-1B employers (table 2.3)—con-

---

24. 28 million workers in the United Kingdom versus 144 million in the United States, according to OECD labor-market data.

25. All data are from ATSCO (2006, 2007).

26. ATSCO (2007) shows that issuance of new IT work permits in the United Kingdom more than doubled by 2006 from just 12,726 in 2000.

27. See page on Frequently Asked Questions on Foreign Labor Certification Prevailing Wages at www.foreignlaborcert.doleta.gov/wages.cfm.

28. Until the Omnibus FY2005 Appropriations bill (HR 4818), which raised it to 100 percent, the "prevailing wage" was legally defined as only 95 percent of what US workers earned. See Kirkegaard (2005) for data showing that employers made wide use of this loophole.

29. See, for instance, Miano (2007) or Hira (2007).

30. See USCIS press release, USCIS Implements L-1 Visa Reform Act of 2004, June 23, 2005, at www.uscis.gov.

cerning 607 H-1B workers who had not been paid prevailing wages during 2004–05.[31] More such targeted enforcement of existing laws would seem the appropriate answer to any concerns over possible underpayment by IT services companies of foreign high-skilled H-1B workers.

Matching Employers with Foreign High-Skilled Workers

Thanks to internet-based job searches and advertising, high-skilled workers, employers, and other potential foreign employees rarely face overwhelming informational obstacles in "matching each other in a labor market" across international borders. This is particularly so in the United States and other English-speaking nations (but also to a lesser degree in French- and Spanish-speaking nations). English is the lingua franca of international business, and a substantial potential pool of English-speaking foreign high-skilled workers exists outside US borders. For high-skilled workers, the principal practical obstacle to cross-border labor-market matching is immigration laws. The degree to which a country's laws choose to accommodate (or not) this relatively easy high-skilled cross-border labor-market matching is a straightforward immigration policy choice.

As mentioned in chapter 1, immigration flows that are family-based, humanitarian, and illegal in nature are of limited high-skilled relevance, and immigration policies emphasizing these types of flows—as in the United States presently—relative to employment-related or student-based immigration thus explicitly downplay the importance of the skills component. However, there are also important differences in the way employment (and student)–oriented immigration functions in terms of guiding domestic employers to potential foreign high-skilled recruits.

Employers in the OECD are generally free to transfer top foreign researchers and executives to a particular country, as is done via the US L-1 visa program. Employers are hence free to manage entirely on their own the cross-border selection of this particular group of high-skilled workers. Alternatively, countries utilize a range of criteria, such as educational qualifications (similar to the requirement in the US H-1B system of at least a bachelor's degree or equivalent), salary levels, or a government-provided list of "occupations with labor shortage" or quotas (like the annual 65,000 H-1B visa cap in America).

Several, especially other Anglo-Saxon, countries utilize so-called points systems, where foreign workers can qualify for a work permit if they obtain a certain number of points, based on a government-issued and usually skills-oriented criteria list. A major advantage of the points system

---

31. See Department of Labor press release dated June 7, 2007, at www.dol.gov/opa/media/press/esa.

is its flexibility, as it can, in theory, be relatively easily calibrated to target particular categories of foreign skills needed at a particular time in the national labor market. Targeted foreign workers can subsequently "self select" and apply of their own initiative or even choose to upgrade their skills prior to applying, should it be required to meet the threshold. Points systems are inherently more focused on skill levels than, say, family-based immigration systems and hence are preferable for alleviating skill shortages.

However, points systems also have drawbacks. As laid out in OECD (2007c, 97ff), their efficient operation requires a substantial and expensive apparatus for verifying foreign-earned credentials and diplomas. Also, points systems frequently substitute educational attainment and degrees for actual skills and qualifications demanded by employers. While any degree holder will be preferred in skill terms to one with no degree, a points system nonetheless runs the risk of facilitating immigration of high-skilled workers—say, liberal arts graduates—less employable than those graduates possessing skills, say, in the science and engineering fields, directly sought by employers. Hence, in terms of labor-market efficiency, a system—like the US H-1B (and L-1)—that allows employers themselves to directly locate, screen, and ultimately via an employer-sponsored work visa hire foreign high-skilled workers is preferable in labor-market efficiency terms to a points-based high-skilled immigration system.

The use of quotas for high-skilled immigration purposes is invariably the worst possible approach from the perspective of labor-market efficiency. It is basic trade economics that quotas imply an inescapable efficiency loss. Moreover, in immigration, their use raises the issue that the number of permits legislatively permitted—like the *rhetorical* 65,000 H-1B cap in the United States—is set ex ante, while actual labor-market needs are ascertained ex post.[32] So even if politicians set a high-skilled worker quota based on objective demand criteria rather than exogenous political pressures, which is extremely unlikely, they would still be overwhelmingly likely to get it badly wrong. The initial H-1B cap was set at 65,000 in the Immigration and Nationality Act of 1990 based at least partly on earlier years' high-skilled worker inflows, and it has returned to this level in FY2004. The H-1B program is a clear example of demand-supply mismatch: In the spring of 2007, the entire quota for FY2008 was used up in less than a day![33]

Another example of the nonsensical use of prefixed quotas for high-skilled visas is the special H-1B carve-outs (see below) that Chile and Singapore received with their free trade agreements (FTAs) with the United

---

32. See OECD (2007c, 97ff) for an elaboration of this sequencing issue.

33. See USCIS press release, USCIS Runs Random Selection Process for H-1Bs, April 13, 2007 (revised), at www.uscis.gov. The technicalities of this oversubscription are discussed later.

States. These two countries get "first choice" of a total of 6,800 H-1B visas annually (or more than 10 percent of the total). If nationals of the two countries do not use the entire quota of these 6,800 visas, also referred to as H-1B1, then the remaining roll over to the initial "open pool" of 58,200 in the following fiscal year. In FY2006 nationals of Chile and Singapore used only 700—just 10 percent—of the 6,800 H-1B visas that their trade negotiators secured for them.[34] Certainly this system works wonderfully for US employers of high-skilled Chileans and Singaporeans, who are guaranteed an H-1B visa should they apply. However, while it is unclear just what concessions the two countries had to give during the FTA negotiations in exchange for their quota carve-outs, the 10 to 1 mismatch between the quota and its actual use amply illustrates the difficulties of predicting ex ante the correct size of a high-skilled visa quota. A similar situation can be seen with the E-3 high-skilled visas for Australian nationals, of which 10,500 were made available in late 2005 based on the US-Australia FTA.[35] In 2006, the first full year the quota was in force, just 1,918 "Australian specialty occupation professionals" were issued visas—i.e., less than a fifth of the available number of visas![36]

Moreover, the bottleneck of a quota creates adverse incentives and harmful uncertainty for business planning. With the economic future evidently always uncertain, companies that most depend on foreign workers will rationally seek to acquire as many visas under the quota as possible—"visa hoarding" is the rational response to this scarce resource—both to guarantee their own access to foreign high-skilled workers and to deny that access to their competitors. It is therefore no surprise that several Indian (and US) IT-related companies dominate the H-1B program. They simply have the most at stake and the biggest economic interest in acquiring these visas.

---

34. See USCIS press release, USCIS Reaches H-1B Cap, June 1, 2006 at www.uscis.gov. Subsequently, 6,100 of the two countries' FY2006 quota were allocated to the open pool of 58,200 in FY2007 for an initial total of 64,300.

35. The law was publicized in the *Federal Register* on September 2, 2005. Unlike the FTAs with Singapore and Chile, the US-Australia FTA has, following the congressional turf war over this issue, no direct mention of the high-skilled immigration issue. Indeed, a side letter to the agreement specifically states that "no provision in it shall be construed to impose any obligation on a party regarding its immigration measures." See the side letter on immigration in chapter 10 of the final text of the US-Australia FTA, available at the USTR website, www.ustr. gov. This side letter is merely a legal fig leaf, aimed at pleasing the US Congress to make it appear that there is no link between FTAs and US immigration law. The *Federal Register* on September 2, 2005 announced the new rule, following an amendment to the Immigration and Nationality Act of 1990 attached to the Emergency Supplemental Appropriations Act for Defense, the Global War on Terror, and Tsunami Relief, 2005, Public Law 109-12 119 Stat. 231, which created the E-3 visa *only* for Australians.

36. Children or spouses of specialty occupation recipients took 1,053 E-3 visas in 2006. See Department of State (2006, table XVI (B)).

Hence, such companies are likely to mobilize substantial economic resources toward this goal. Stuart Anderson (2006) in testimony before the US Congress estimated that each H-1B visa today costs up to $5,000 to $6,000, depending on whether employers pay the $1,000 "premium processing fee." Infosys, the top user of H-1B visas (table 2.3), stated the following in its 2007 20-F filing:

> In addition, the availability of visas for working in the United States may vary substantially from quarter to quarter. Visas for working in the United States may be available during one quarter, but not another, or there may be differences in the number of visas available from one quarter to another. As such, the variable availability of visas may require us to incur significantly higher visa-related expenses in certain quarters when compared to others. For example, we incurred $11.0 million in costs for visas in the three months ended June 30, 2006, compared to $3.0 million for the three months ended March 31, 2006. Such fluctuations may affect our operating margins and profitability in certain quarters during a fiscal year.[37]

With Infosys and likely most other companies at the top of the H-1B usage list literally spending millions of dollars each quarter on securing these visas, potentially interested US employers with less financial resources to pay immigration lawyers and fees—such as most US startups and small and medium-sized enterprises—are certain to lose out in accessing foreign high-skilled talent.

Perversely, one might argue that an "H-1B auction system" has inadvertently been established such that only those companies with the greatest economic interest in acquiring H-1B workers may do so in reality. In some respects such an implicit H-1B auction system would be economically efficient but begs the question why the US Citizenship and Immigration Service (USCIS) and immigration lawyers should reap the majority of the proceeds from such an auction?

Such H-1B auction rents are far from negligible. Through current visa regulations, the USCIS estimates that in FY2006 it "earned" $138 million in annual fee revenue.[38] The Omnibus FY2005 Appropriations bill (HR 4818) earmarks $1,500 per application as a "retraining fee,[39] which goes toward US workers, and $500 as an "antifraud fee," which goes toward enforcement activities. However, these data include only the 85,000 fully fee-earning H-1B visas processed annually under the congressional cap.

---

37. Available at the Securities and Exchange Commission's EDGAR database for company information at www.sec.gov/edgar.

38. Based on 85,000 fee-paying petitions. The Office of Management and Budget (OMB Circular no. A-25 on "User Charges") demands that federal agencies charge "full cost" of providing special benefits to a recipient when calculating fees. Full cost is defined as "all direct and indirect costs to any part of the Federal Government of providing a good, resource or service." See Gonzalez (2007) and GAO (2005).

39. It is $750 for companies employing fewer than 25 full-time employees.

Yet, table 2.1 showed that in FY2005, more than 267,000 H-1B visas were issued when all categories are included. This implies that when viewed from the perspective of US-based employers—who ultimately pay the bills—the total annual costs of acquiring H-1B visas may have approached $1 billion in FY2005.

A "back-of-the-envelope" estimate, based on Anderson (2006), for total costs of $5,000 per visa for the 85,000 visas under the FY2005 cap and $3,000 for all 182,000 visas granted that did not count toward the cap in FY2005 (which means that they wereexempt from the fees mentioned above) equals total costs in the $1 billion range.[40] As currently implemented, the H-1B cap thus clearly favors highly H-1B dependent Indian IT companies and (as usual) US lawyers.

Given this cost level for US businesses, it is ironic that the USCIS in April 2007, following the receipt of more than 123,400 H-1B applications on April 2–3, introduced a lottery (or in USCIS language, "computer-generated random selection process") to distribute the 65,000 visas available in FY2007.[41] While in some respects perhaps legally fair, such a lottery approach is without doubt the least economically efficient way to match employers and foreign high-skilled workers.

---

40. GAO (2005) indicates that US businesses may spend more than $100 million on accessing the 20,000 H-1B visas available to foreign recipients of master's degrees or higher at US universities.

41. See USCIS press release, Change in H-1B Procedures Trims Weeks off Final Selection Process, April 19, 2007, at www.uscis.gov. April 1, 2007 was a Sunday, and hence the USCIS started receiving petitions only on April 2. The agency did not notify the public until April 3 that the cap of 65,000 had been reached (USCIS press release, USCIS Reaches FY2008 H-1B Cap, April 3, 2007), and it was subsequently administratively determined that all petitions filed prior hereto had been legally received on the "final receipt day."

4

A Reform Package

The recent debate in America on immigration reform has failed to pay sufficient attention to several accelerating trends in immigration of high-skilled workers. While legislated, the US high-skilled immigration system has been largely left unreformed and has become increasingly dysfunctional. US policymakers must urgently acknowledge the accelerating trends, summarized below, before they produce a crisis.

Summary of Findings

This policy analysis has established the following findings:

The Era of Rising Skill Levels in America's Labor Force Is Drawing to a Close. Overall skill levels in the US workforce have stagnated in the last 30 years. Measured by educational attainment, new cohorts of workforce entrants aged 25–29 and 30–34 do not possess higher skills than soon-to-retire baby boomers aged 55–59. This indicates that the qualitative, compositional improvement of the skill level in the US labor force associated with the retirement of workers less skilled than those entering will stop for the first time in US history. Retiring baby boomers will take as many skills with them into retirement as their children simultaneously entering the workforce possess.

The Number of High-Skilled Workers in Other Countries Is Rising Faster than in America. American baby boomers aged 55–64 led the global economy in tertiary education when they entered the workforce in the 1970s. Today's American workforce entrants aged 25–34 barely make the global top 10, signifying that America will soon start dropping down the list of nations with the most skilled workforces. At least ten percentage points more of young workforce entrants in Russia, Canada, Japan, and Korea today have a tertiary degree than does the present share of youngsters in America. This indicates that present and future generations of Americans may not possess the same relative skill advantages to thrive in the global economy as did Americans aged 55+.

Science and Engineering Degrees Are Still Popular. Measured as a share of the total number of bachelor's, master's, and doctoral degrees granted by US universities, science and engineering (S&E) degrees have held largely steady at least since the mid-1970s. Shortages of new S&E graduates are thus related more to the general educational stagnation in the United States than to any relative decline in popularity of these fields.

Foreign Science and Engineering Students Have Been Numerous at US Universities for a Generation. The foreign share of US S&E students rose substantially during the 1990s and has now stabilized at more than a third after a 9/11-related decline. More than half of all engineering and computer science students at US universities in 2005 were foreign. However, as far back as the 1980s, this share was 40 percent or more.

OECD Countries Are Increasingly Shifting Toward Managed Immigration, Focusing More on High Skills than Is America. In 2005 the United States had the most family-oriented immigration policy of the 17 OECD countries for which data were available. Many OECD countries, including those outside the group of traditional Anglo-Saxon immigrant destination countries, are aggressively courting high-skilled immigrants and especially copying US efforts to attract foreign students and provide them with employment opportunities. Moreover, traditional origin countries of many high-skilled emigrants to the United States, like China, have in 2007 actively begun luring their nationals back via special offers. This raises the question whether the United States can retain its large share of all foreign high-skilled immigrants and maintain its traditionally very high retention rate among its foreign student body.

High-Skilled Immigrants Are Increasingly Important as US High-Tech Entrepreneurs. Up to 25 percent of all US high-tech startups since the early 1990s have had at least one foreign-born cofounder. This share is an increase from less than 10 percent in the 1970s.

Green Cards Keep High-Skilled Foreigners in the United States, but Don't Grant Them Entrance. More than 90 percent of the green cards (i.e., the granting of legal permanent residence [LPR] status) to high-skilled immigrants are issued via adjustments in visa status requested for high-skilled foreigners already residing and (most likely) employed in the United States. Green cards are thus important predominantly as a tool to maintain the existing high-skilled workforce in the United States, rather than expanding it. This indicates that temporary visas perform a "gatekeeping" function for most high-skilled permanent immigrants to the United States and that overwhelmingly it is temporary work visas, rather than green cards, that in the first place attract "the best and the brightest" to the United States.

The Present Green Card System May Force Many Employed High-Skilled Workers to Leave the United States. Due to the limited number of green cards that can be issued to any single country's nationals, most high-skilled immigrants from China, India, and the Philippines have had to wait several years to be able to acquire permanent residency in the United States. Such national bottlenecks in the green card system may force many of them to abandon high-skilled US employment and leave the US workforce.

The Current Cap on Annual H-1B Issuance Is Pure Political Rhetoric. More than 275,000 H-1B visas were issued in FY2004 and FY2005, despite the cap being nominally set at 65,000. This is a direct and intentional result of congressionally mandated legal exceptions and is unrelated to large-scale visa fraud.

A Dual Trend Dominates Temporary High-Skilled Visa Issuance in the L-1 and H-1B Programs, and Indians Now Dominate Both. The issuance of H-1B and L-1 visas to Indian nationals has rapidly increased in recent years, so that Indians now account for 30 to 50 percent of all temporary high-skilled visas issued, depending on the subcategory. Visa issuance to nationals from the rest of the world has been largely stagnant since 2000. More detailed occupational data for H-1B recipients show that the gross number of Indian recipients, recipients in computer-related occupations, and recipients in the IT services sectors fluctuates wildly and broadly as would be directionally predicted by the business cycle. Gross H-1B visa issuance to other recipient categories is generally stable. Foreign high-skilled workers in computer-related occupations in all probability increasingly dominate both programs.

New Firm-Level Data on L-1 and H-1B Usage for 2006 Show a Limited Number of Indian IT Companies at the Very Top. Recent data released by Senators Richard Durbin and Charles Grassley on employers that request L-1 and H-1B visas show that up to a dozen Indian IT services/software companies were the top petitioners of L-1 and H-1B visas in 2006. Several major US IT companies are also heavy users of the two programs.

However, Indian IT services/software companies do not feature beyond the top 10. Instead, a very broad range of US and multinational companies, as well as US public institutions from different sectors of the US economy, account for the remaining demand for foreign high-skilled workers. Firm-level data thus confirm the importance of both the L-1 and H-1B visas to the IT services/software industries and a few Indian companies in particular, while simultaneously indicating a broad-based demand for foreign high-skilled workers throughout the US economy.

US Software Workers Have Not Been Adversely Affected by the Uniquely Large Inflow of Foreign High-Skilled Workers in this Occupation. No other high-skilled occupation in the United States has seen an inflow of foreign workers that approaches that of software workers. Yet, numerous media reports and congressional testimony notwithstanding, unemployment rates for both US computer programmers and software engineers have hovered around 2 percent since 2005, indicating full employment in these occupations. Latest available data show total software employment was at a record high in 2006, surpassing the level reached at the peak of the internet/Y2K boom.

Wage growth for US software workers has in recent years surpassed that for 80 percent of the US workforce. This further suggests that US high-skilled workers have not suffered adverse labor-market effects by the inflow of foreign high-skilled workers in recent years. It is therefore crucial that nonempirical alarmist rhetoric and anecdotes not be allowed to dominate the public discourse on this topic in America, as these will likely have an unwarranted negative effect on the willingness of US students to pursue careers in software occupations.

The Use of Quotas for H-1B Visas May Generate up to $1 Billion in Annual Rents in the Form of Fees to the USCIS and Immigration Lawyers. Turning access to H-1B visas into a scarce resource through the use of a quota heavily favors the most resource-rich and intensive/dependent users of the program, likely at the expense of smaller US startups and small and medium-sized companies.

Implications and Recommendations for Reform

Any reform of US immigration laws is today more than ever "politics as the art of the possible" rather than the ideal. As even successful education reforms take decades to yield marked skill improvements in the labor market, it should be noncontroversial that the United States will need to increase its intake of high-skilled foreigners to avoid substantial and broad skill shortages in the coming decade. Hence, the current overwhelming emphasis on family-based immigration must be altered in the direction of a more skills-oriented approach. However, accepting that such fundamental redirection of US immigration policies invariably will touch upon areas and issues outside the subjects relevant to high-skilled immigration covered in this policy analysis, I will refrain from proposing sweeping reforms toward this broader goal.

Keeping in mind the current political sensitivity of the issue, most recently exemplified by the collapse of the June 2007 Senate immigration "grand compromise," I instead offer a package of minimalist policy proposals—i.e., biased in favor of changes that are most necessary but require only the least ambitious legislative agenda. Proposing limited reforms is also acknowledging the fact that despite its increasing number of shortcomings, the US high-skilled immigration system does contain many well-functioning and efficient rules and regulations, altered at lawmakers' peril.

Permanent Immigration—Green Card Issuance

The present green card system generally functions reasonably well with respect to high-skilled workers and ought to carry on with its current function as the principal means with which to keep the best and the brightest in the United States rather than attract them. The findings in this policy analysis suggest that, apart from speeding up the processing of LPR applications, two changes to current rules should be made:

Drop the Department of Labor (DOL) Foreign Labor Certification for LPR Categories E-2 and E-3. The US labor force will shortly start experiencing a stagnation in the skill level of the resident workforce, leaving the resident high-skilled workers unaffected by foreign high-skilled inflows. Hence the current requirement that foreigners seeking LPR status in categories E-2 and E-3 obtain a labor-market certification is superfluous and will only lead to rent-seeking behavior.

Exempt LPR Categories E-1, E-2, and E-3 from the Annual Per-Country National Limit. High-skilled foreigners from many different origins seek LPR status via the E-2 and E-3 categories, but the population sizes of countries vary widely. Recent evidence shows that literally hundreds of thousands of would-be permanent residents from China, India, and the Philippines applied for LPR status immediately when offered the chance in July and August 2007. Moreover, up to 40 percent of the world's population is already from either India or China, and the pool of high-skilled university graduates from these two countries is expanding rapidly every year. It no longer makes any sense to restrict the number of high-skilled people who can annually enter the United States from any one country.

L-1 Intracompany Transferees

The L-1 visa program grants employers utmost freedom to independently select which foreign high-skilled workers they require and bring them to the United States without having to concern themselves with visa quotas, labor certifications, or other regulatory obstacles. This is a very efficient program, which lets employers identify and access the precise foreign high-skilled workers they need. As such, no major specific reforms of the L-1 program are presently required.

However, the L-1 program has seen a major rise in applications filed on behalf of Indian nationals and is very intensively used by a very small group of Indian and US IT services/software companies. This finding broadly mirrors that for the H-1B program, and the appropriate, integrated policy response is covered in the next subsection.

H-1B Specialty Occupations

The H-1B program, similar to the L-1 program, allows employers in the United States the freedom to identify the foreign workers who possess the skills they most require. This aspect of the H-1B program should be maintained, but several others need to be reformed.

Drop the DOL Foreign Labor Certification for H-1B Workers. This policy analysis has shown that despite the uniquely large inflows of high-skilled foreigners in computer-related occupations in recent years, US software workers in the aggregate have not suffered in the US labor market. Given that no other job occupation has seen inflows of the same magnitude and is thus extremely unlikely to have suffered as a result of such foreign inflows, the foreign labor certification for H-1B workers is unnecessary. When full employment exists in an occupation, there is no further economic or labor-market reason to demand that employers explicitly attempt to hire US workers before bringing in a foreign high-skilled worker. Considering the large additional administrative costs for companies—application filing fees, attorneys' fees, time value of postponed hiring, etc.—it seems highly unlikely that any company would at prevailing wages seek to hire a foreign worker ahead of an American if the two possessed otherwise identical skill sets.

Increase, Unshackle, and Target Enforcement of Prevailing Wages to Intensive Users of H-1B Visas. H-1B workers must be paid prevailing US wages as determined only by the DOL, and, given the very high concentration of H-1B workers at a relatively small number of companies, the appropriate way to do so is through unrestricted DOL enforcement of this provision.[1]

Abolish the Annual Congressional Cap for H-1B Visas. With high-skilled green cards overwhelmingly going to aliens already inside the United States, it is imperative that the "doorway of initial entry"—i.e., temporary high-skilled visas that attract the best and the brightest—be kept wide open. Visa quotas are inherently arbitrary, if not explicitly politically manipulated in size, and invariably lead to large efficiency losses. Moreover, this policy analysis has shown that the share of H-1B visas that go to initial employment (i.e., count towards the cap) in noncomputer-related occupations is relatively stable at about 65,000 to 75,000 in total during 2000–2005 (the period for which data are available). Given this stability and variety in noncomputer-related demand for H-1B visas, it is unlikely that abolishing the congressional cap will lead to a massive instantaneous increase in demand for visas, and hence the cap is unnecessary. Alternatively, a "de facto nonbinding cap" deliberately set at a sufficiently high level that would not be approached under normal economic circumstances—say, 500,000 annually—could be maintained in the books as a legal safety guard.

Abolish the Annual 20,000 Congressional Cap and Grant Automatic H-1B Visas to Interested Foreign Master's and Doctoral Graduates from US Universities. With rising shares of foreign students, especially in S&E fields, and increasing global competition for international students, it makes less sense than ever to prevent foreign high-skilled students, educated in America, usually supported by US tax-benefited university scholarships, from obtaining employment in the United States. The current situation is such that the 20,000 H-1B visas available for FY2008 were exhausted on May 4, 2007—i.e., prior to university graduations this year. Unless a foreign student graduating in 2007 has one year of optional practical training (OPT) available, he or she will be effectively barred from seeking employment in the US for-profit sector.[2] Interested foreign recipients of master's and doctoral degrees from US universities with a US employer petitioning on their behalf should be guaranteed access to an H-1B visa.

---

1. In April 2007 Senators Durbin and Grassley sensibly suggested giving "the DOL the ability to conduct random audits of any company that uses the H-1B program, and would require DOL to conduct annual audits of companies with more than 100 employees that have 15% or more of those workers on H-1B visas." See Durbin and Grassley Introduce First Bipartisan H-1B Visa Reform Bill to Protect American Workers, April 2, 2009, available at http://durbin.senate.gov.

2. See USCIS press release, USCIS Reaches Exemption Cap for Fiscal Year 2008, May 4, 2007, available at www.uscis.gov.

Restrict the Share of Foreign High-Skilled Workers that a Single Business Entity over a Certain Size Can Employ on Temporary Work Visas— i.e., Including Both H-1B and L-1—to a Sensible Level. The H-1B and L-1 programs were designed to allow US employers to identify foreign high-skilled workers and bring them to America, as economic circumstances dictated, to supplement resident workers. This policy analysis has established that instead a very small number of Indian and US IT services/ software companies seem to use these temporary work visa programs as a way to sustain an on-site delivery model in the United States, overwhelmingly staffed by foreign high-skilled workers in the IT services/software sector. While perfectly legal, this use of the H-1B and L-1 visa programs is scopewise unintended. In order to politically safeguard these programs for their original beneficial and increasingly necessary economic function, this novel use should be curbed. Such actions of a handful of IT companies, though completely legal, must not hold the entire US high-skilled immigration debate hostage. These actions can be curbed, for instance, as suggested by Senators Durbin and Grassley in April 2007, by prohibiting companies with over 50 workers from employing more than a 50 percent share of foreign workers on H-1B, or L-1, work visas.[3]

Such a restriction would affect only a very limited number of Indian and US IT services/software companies and not concern any major household US IT company. Moreover, as stated by Tata Consultancy Services head of global human resources S. "Paddy" Padmanabhan, in a May 2007 interview with technology weekly *InformationWeek*,[4] 99 percent of the company's high-skilled workers on temporary H-1B visas leave the United States upon visa expiry, rather than pursue a green card. This indicates that limiting the number of temporary visas available to this group of IT services/software companies will not jeopardize the flow of high-skilled workers seeking permanent US residency.

Strike a Bilateral Immigration Agreement with India and Create a New Visa Category for Workers in the IT Services/Software Sector. Undoubtedly, the above proposal to restrict the share of foreign high-skilled workers that any but the smallest company can hire will, based on firm-level data presented in this policy analysis, disproportionately affect Indian IT

---

3. Senators Durbin and Grassley suggested that the threshold be 50 workers, and 50 percent of the workforce could be on H-1B visas alone and not include L-1 visas. See Durbin and Grassley Introduce First Bipartisan H-1B Visa Reform Bill to Protect American Workers, April 2, 2007, available at http://durbin.senate.gov.

4. See Chris Murphy and Marianne Kolbasuk McGee, "Majority Of U.S. Staffers At Indian Outsourcers Are On H-1B Visas," *InformationWeek*, May 15, 2007, available at www.informationweek.com.

services companies and Indian nationals.[5] Via their intensive use of the L-1 and H-1B visa programs to sustain their on-site delivery business models, these companies are benefiting from a novel way to utilize the current US temporary high-skilled immigration system. However, as already mentioned, this benefit has accrued to Indian IT services/software companies and their US clones largely though a new, unintended, and—crucially— politically unsustainable use of these US high-skilled visa programs.

Considering that the US market accounts for up to two-thirds of Indian IT exports, worth up to $10 billion in 2007,[6] the present level of access to temporary US high-skilled visas is of substantial value to the Indian economy. In some respects, this benefit has been at least partly acquired by legally gaming the existing US temporary high-skilled immigration system, indirectly at the expense of other potential US-based users of available visas. The US Congress should overcome jurisdictional turf wars between trade negotiators and immigration officials[7] and realize the negotiating value temporary high-skilled work visas hold today in negotiations with India. In return for appropriate Indian policy concessions—for instance, as a major pillar in a US-India free trade agreement (FTA)—the United States should agree to establish an entirely new visa category— say, "IT visa"—that would be applicable to high-skilled Indian workers in computer-related occupations.

An IT visa for Indian nationals would follow a string of bilateral deals made by US trade negotiators concerning high-skilled visas in recent years. Australia got an annual quota of 10,500 high-skilled E-3 visas as part of its FTA negotiations with the United States.[8] Chile[9] and Singapore got quotas of 1,400 and 5,600 H-1B visas, respectively, of the annual 65,000

---

5. It should be noted that many of the main Indian IT companies—Tata Consultancy Services, Infosys, and Wipro being the three biggest—are currently recruiting increasingly aggressively across the world, including at US campuses. As such, their stated business strategies to become truly global multinational companies will at the same time gradually make them less dependent on Indian nationals in their workforces. These companies have grown rapidly from their Indian bases in just the last decade. Turning into truly global services companies—say, like IBM—will take time but nonetheless will gradually make them less dependent on US work visas and other "export markets" for Indian nationals.

6. Data are from NASSCOM (2007). Much uncertainty surrounds the precise dollar level of Indian IT services exports, but what is not in doubt is that the United States is India's largest market.

7. See, for instance, the May 2005 letter from then House Judiciary Committee Chairman F. James Sensenbrenner, Jr. and Ranking Member John Conyers, Jr. to then US Trade Representative Robert Portman, insisting that the administration not include immigration provisions in trade deals that require changes in US laws (*Inside US Trade,* June 1, 2007, 3).

8. See US embassy in Australia, "E-3 Visas," http://canberra.usembassy.gov.

9. See US embassy in Chile, "Nonimmigrant Visas," http://santiago.usembassy.gov.

quota as part of their FTAs with the United States. Canadian and Mexican citizens, as part of the North American Free Trade Agreement (NAFTA), became eligible for work in the United States as nonimmigrant NAFTA professionals,[10] provided that their profession is on the NAFTA list of eligible professions and that they possess the required skills.[11] A bilateral high-skilled visa agreement with India, however, would be "the big one" and carry a correspondingly large bargaining-chip significance in any potential US-India FTA negotiations.

An IT visa for Indians would be an appropriate response to the on-site delivery business model pioneered to scale by Indian IT services/software companies. It would further be a partial recognition of the new international factor mobility in the services sectors, initially indicated by the General Agreement on Trade in Services (GATS) mode 4—the cross-border supply of a service by a country's service suppliers through the presence of natural persons in the territory of another country. Quite a large literature exists on the broader topic of the "GATS visa," which would presumably be multilateral in nature and horizontal—i.e., cover all services sectors.[12] In 2003 14 developing countries, including India, submitted such a proposal for liberalizing mode 4 as part of the GATS negotiations.[13]

This proposed bilateral US-India IT visa would be far more limited in nature and cover only Indian nationals with at least a bachelor's degree and employed at prevailing US wages at a company with a contract to perform IT services/software-related work in the United States. It would be open to both employees at contractual service suppliers and independent professionals. Such a visa would be temporary only and perhaps be valid initially for up to two years and renewable as required.

More broadly, it seems clear that trade relations via mode 4—i.e., through the on-site delivery model—will increasingly spread to other sec-

---

10. See US Department of State, "Mexican and Canadian NAFTA Professional Worker," http://travel.state.gov.

11. See NAFTA website for complete list of eligible occupations and required skills at www.nafta-sec-alena.org. It has also been suggested that Korea, as part of the final negotiations of its FTA with the United States, should seek an H-1B carve-out similar to that of Chile and Singapore. Its outcome is, however, at present unknown. See *Inside US Trade*, June 1, 2007, 3.

12. For an overview of this literature, see, for instance, the conference papers from the two World Trade Organization (WTO)–hosted conferences in Geneva in 2002 and 2004: Movement of natural persons (mode 4) under the GATS, Joint WTO–World Bank Symposium, Geneva, April 11–12, 2002; and Managing the Movement of People: What can be learned for Mode 4 of the GATS? Joint IOM/World Bank/WTO Seminar, Geneva, October 4–5, 2004, available at www.wto.org.

13. See WTO document TN/S/W/14, July 3, 2003. The 14 participating countries include most of the potential large origin countries for high-skilled service-sector workers: Argentina, Bolivia, Chile, China, Colombia, Dominican Republic, Egypt, Guatemala, India, Mexico, Pakistan, Peru, Philippines, and Thailand. Available at http://commerce.nic.in/trade.

tors than IT services. It would therefore be fortuitous if US immigration laws moved in a direction that gradually facilitated this trend.

The proposed "IT visa" would not—unlike the L-1 and H-1B visa categories—have a dual intent clause, and hence it would not be possible for "IT visa" holders to apply for US legal permanent resident status while inside the United States on this visa status. Hence it would facilitate Indian nationals to return to India upon visa expiration and pave the way for the formation of a sustained "brain chain" (not brain drain) of talent exchange between the United States and India. Given the serious skilled-labor constraints indicated by the rampant IT skilled-worker wage inflation in India, such a "brain chain" will make this visa agreement more valuable to India by preventing large-scale IT skills hemorrhaging. As such, the proposed IT visa will be in direct accordance with the mandate of the Indian government's High Level Committee on Indian Diaspora, which since 2003 has been tasked with "facilitating diaspora interaction with India and their participation in India's economic development."[14]

The main concerns of any business-oriented visa are generally transparency, expediency, and minimal burdensomeness, yielding a visa-wise predictable business environment for companies. Such predictability is definitely required in the IT services industry, where flexible, timely onsite delivery capacity is an important competitive parameter. Hence, the use—as in other bilateral US visa agreements—of quotas must be completely avoided. The number of available US-India IT visas would be uncapped but instead carry an explicit price tag per visa.

Considering that this policy analysis has shown how IT companies today routinely spend millions of dollars each quarter to secure an adequate number of H-1B and L-1 visas, it would not seem far-fetched, in return for guaranteed (limiting the need for immigration lawyers) and expedient (say, a two-week maximum processing time) high-skilled visa issuance, to put the price in the $7,500 to $10,000+ range per high-skilled IT visa.

From such an IT visa, Indian businesses and nationals would gain assured access to the US market. Indeed, the president of India's National Association of Software and Service Companies (NASSCOM), Kiran Karnik, has pleaded several times for precisely this type of visa.[15] Visa revenue from this IT visa could be directly channeled to improving retraining opportunities for US workers—as is being done in the H-1B visa program via retraining fees. At the same time, the "visa markup" applied to high-skilled Indian IT workers' prevailing wages would insulate similarly skilled US software workers against displacement. Lastly, the DOL would

---

14. See the mandate of the High Level Committee on Indian Diaspora at http://indiadiaspora. nic.in/mandate.htm.

15. See Karnik's comments in "Nasscom Moots Visas for Onsite Assignments," *Hindu Business Line*, April 27, 2003, available at the NASSCOM website, www.nasscom.in.

enforce the IT visa in a manner similar to the regular H-1B program.

Regularly Publish Official Firm-Level Immigration Data and Detailed Data on the Characteristics of All High-Skilled Immigrants. High-skilled immigration should be driven by an economy's skill requirements and the characteristics of both the employers and the high-skilled immigrants themselves. For high-skilled immigration to occur as seamlessly as possible, a high level of transparency is in the public interest. This need for transparency is accentuated by the privileged immigration status granted to high-skilled immigrants relative to other immigrants, as well as by the need to frequently dispel populist and protectionist misrepresentations of the scale, character, and impact of high-skilled immigration.

Statistical Appendix

Table A.1 Educational attainment of the US population 15 years and older, by age, 2006 (thousands)

Age group[a]	Total	None	1st–4th grade	5th–6th grade	7th–8th grade	9th grade	10th grade	11th grade[b]
15 and over	233,194	996	2,119	3,950	7,857	8,576	9,891	13,574
15 to 17	13,344	19	15	41	2,352	4,245	4,128	2,337
18 to 19	7,572	7	20	27	106	168	440	2,463
20 to 24	20,393	31	72	216	274	408	473	1,224
25 to 29	20,138	50	129	384	320	447	445	959
30 to 34	19,343	60	120	389	317	390	359	775
35 to 39	20,771	88	165	409	289	376	366	805
40 to 44	22,350	88	142	394	341	338	480	836
45 to 49	22,518	87	153	316	355	369	485	759
50 to 54	20,279	77	165	350	315	292	434	734
55 to 59	17,827	76	145	246	394	239	402	494
60 to 64	13,153	73	167	182	354	266	393	503
65 to 69	10,231	57	198	210	462	273	336	457
70 to 74	8,323	66	215	218	480	204	323	405
75 and over	16,951	217	414	568	1,496	562	828	823
18 and over	219,849	977	2,104	3,910	5,505	4,331	5,763	11,237
15 to 24	41,309	57	107	283	2,732	4,821	5,041	6,025
25 and over	191,884	939	2,012	3,667	5,124	3,755	4,850	7,549
15 to 64	197,689	656	1,293	2,954	5,418	7,537	8,404	11,888
65 and over	35,505	340	827	996	2,438	1,039	1,487	1,686

— = represents zero or rounds to zero

a. All races and both sexes.

b. 12th grade, no diploma are included in this category.

Note: Civilian noninstitutionalized population plus armed forces living off post or with their families on post. Aggregated data based on sex, race, and Hispanic origin.

Source: US Census Bureau and Bureau of Labor Statistics, Current Population Survey, 2006 Annual Social and Economic Supplement, available at www.census.gov (accessed in September 2007).

High school graduate	Some college, no degree	Associate's degree, occupa- tional	Associate's degree, academic	Bachelor's degree	Master's degree	Profes- sional degree	Doctoral degree
69,548	42,464	9,444	8,707	37,334	13,184	3,061	2,489
147	52	—	5	3	—	—	1
2,287	2,012	22	12	7	—	2	—
6,216	7,789	660	693	2,171	131	10	24
5,768	4,066	903	948	4,429	988	185	117
5,534	3,477	959	876	4,187	1,420	281	199
6,055	3,506	994	957	4,501	1,594	383	283
7,081	3,741	1,217	1,066	4,588	1,419	374	245
7,340	3,829	1,206	1,201	4,286	1,464	399	269
6,160	3,615	1,055	930	3,827	1,667	369	290
5,414	3,283	858	763	3,237	1,621	305	349
4,511	2,167	538	477	1,945	1,100	217	261
3,752	1,563	322	330	1,317	603	178	172
3,160	1,170	233	166	1,000	415	157	111
6,124	2,194	477	283	1,836	762	202	168
69,401	42,412	9,444	8,702	37,332	13,184	3,061	2,488
8,651	9,853	682	709	2,181	131	11	25
60,898	32,611	8,762	7,998	35,153	13,053	3,050	2,464
56,513	37,537	8,412	7,928	33,182	11,405	2,524	2,038
13,035	4,926	1,032	779	4,153	1,780	538	451

Table A.2 USCIS statistics on successful H-1B petitions, fiscal years 1999–2006

	1999[a] (1)	2000 (2)	2001 (3)	2002 (4)	2003 (5)	2004 (6)	2005 (7)	2006
Petitions for initial employment								
1 Total number of H-1B petitions granted	n.a.	257,640	331,206	197,537	217,340	287,418	267,131	n.a.
2 Of which: Number of H-1B petitions granted for initial employment (percent of total petitions granted)	134,400 (n.a.)	136,787 (53)	201,787 (61)	103,584 (52)	105,314 (48)	130,497 (45)	116,927 (44)	n.a.
3 Of which: Aliens were outside the United States at the time of employer petition (percent of total initial employment petitions)	81,100 (60)	75,785 (55)	115,759 (57)	36,494 (35)	41,895 (40)	60,271 (46)	54,635 (47)	n.a.
4 Of which: Aliens were inside the United States at the time of employer petition (percent of total initial employment petitions)	53,300 (40)	61,002 (45)	85,320 (43)	67,090 (65)	63,419 (60)	70,226 (54)	62,292 (53)	n.a.
5 Of which: #1 country of origin (percent of total)	India 63,900 (48)	India 60,757 (44)	India 90,668 (45)	India 21,066 (20)	India 29,269 (29)	India 60,062 (46)	India 57,349 (49)	n.a.
6 Of which: #2 country of origin (percent of total)	China 12,400 (9)	China 12,333 (9)	China 16,847 (8)	China 11,832 (11)	China 11,144 (11)	China 11,365 (9)	China 10,643 (9)	n.a.

(table continues next page)

95

Table A.2 USCIS statistics on successful H-1B petitions, fiscal years 1999–2006 (continued)

	1999[a] (1)	2000 (2)	2001 (3)	2002 (4)	2003 (5)	2004 (6)	2005 (7)	2006
7 Of which: #3 country of origin (percent of total)	United Kingdom 4,400 (3)	Canada 5,465(4)	Canada 9,184 (5)	Canada 7,893 (8)	Canada 6,201 (6)	Canada 5,229 (4)	Canada 4,246 (4)	n.a
8 Of which: #1 occupational group (percent of total) and median earnings	n.a.	Computer-related occupations 74,551 (55) $50,000	Computer-related occupations 110,713 (55) $51,600	Computer-related occupations 25,637 (25) $55,000	Computer-related occupations 28,879 (27) $50,500	Computer-related occupations 56,559 (44) $50,000	Computer-related occupations 52,353 (45) $50,000	n.a.
9 Of which: #2 occupational group (percent of total) and median earnings	n.a.	Occupations in architecture, engineering, and surveying 17,086 (12) $51,480	Occupations in architecture, engineering, and surveying 25,365 (13) $56,485	Occupations in architecture, engineering, and surveying 14,467 (14) $52,000	Occupations in education 15,008 (14) $36,000	Occupations in architecture, engineering, and surveying 13,625 (11) $50,000	Occupations in architecture, engineering, and surveying 12,831 (11) $55,000	n.a.
10 Of which: #3 occupational group (percent of total) and median earnings	n.a.	Occupations in administrative specializations 11,468 (8) $38,000	Occupations in administrative specializations 15,573 (8) $40,000	Occupations in education 13,996 (14) $35,000	Occupations in administrative specializations 13,892 (13) $38,900	Occupations in education 13,185 (10) $38,000	Occupations in education 12,978 (11) $39,000	n.a.
11 Of which: Number employed in IT services industry (percent of total)[b]	n.a.	n.a.	88,613 (44)	17,803 (17)	19,347 (19)	47,362 (36)	44,644 (38)	n.a.
12 Of which: Number employed in IT hardware industry (percent of total)[c]	n.a.	n.a.	4,824 (2)	2,210 (2)	1,554 (1)	2,231 (2)	2,549 (2)	n.a.

13	*Addendum*: Number of H-1B visas issued by the US State Department (percent of total H-1B petitions granted)[d]	116,513 (n.a.)	133,290 (52)	161,643 (49)	118,352 (60)	107,196 (49)	138,965 (48)	124,100 (46)	135,421
14	*Addendum*: Number of H-1B visas issued by the US State Department to Indian nationals (percent of total H-1B petitions granted to Indians)	55,062 (n.a.)	61,530 (49)	74,078 (46)	44,012 (68)	42,245 (53)	63,737 (52)	53,579 (45)	64,887
15	*Addendum*: Number of H-1B visas issued by the US State Department to Chinese nationals (percent of total H-1B petitions granted to Chinese)	5,775 (n.a.)	7,489 (33)	9,076 (33)	7,576 (40)	5,608 (28)	6,583 (25)	7,113 (29)	9,451
16	*Addendum*: Number of H-1B visas issued by the US State Department to British nationals	6,664	7,304	8,462	6,842	6,095	6,557	5,617	4,805
17	*Addendum*: H-1B cap	115,000	115,000	195,000	195,000	195,000	65,000	85,000[e]	85,000[e]

(table continues next page)

Table A.2 USCIS statistics on successful H-1B petitions, fiscal years 1999–2006 (continued)

	1999[a]	2000 (8)	2001 (9)	2002 (10)	2003 (11)	2004 (12)	2005 (13)
Petitions for continuing employment							
1 Total number of H-1B petitions granted	n.a.	257,640	331,206	197,537	217,340	287,418	267,131
2 Of which: Number of H-1B petitions granted for continuing employment (percent of total)	n.a.	120,853 (47)	130,127 (39)	93,953 (48)	112,026 (52)	156,921 (55)	149,932 (56)
5 Of which: #1 country of origin (percent of total)	n.a.	India 63,940 (53)	India 70,893 (54)	India 43,914 (47)	India 49,897 (45)	India 63,505 (41)	India 61,171 (41)
6 Of which: #2 country of origin (percent of total)	n.a.	China 10,237 (8)	China 10,483 (8)	China 7,009 (7)	China 8,919 (8)	China 14,893 (10)	China 13,918 (9)
7 Of which: #3 country of origin (percent of total)	n.a.	Canada 2,900(2)	Canada 3,542 (3)	Canada 3,867 (4)	Canada 4,959 (4)	Canada 8,183 (5)	Canada 7,534 (5)
8 Of which: #1 occupational group (percent of total) and median earnings	n.a.	Computer-related occupations 73,875 (61) $65,000	Computer-related occupations 80,684 (62) $69,000	Computer-related occupations 49,477 (53) $64,739	Computer-related occupations 54,235 (48) $63,000	Computer-related occupations 70,720 (45) $65,000	Computer-related occupations 61,515 (41) $68,000
9 Of which: #2 occupational group (percent of total) and median earnings	n.a.	Occupations in architecture, engineering, and surveying 14,298 (12) $65,000	Occupations in architecture, engineering, and surveying 15,023 (12) $68,000	Occupations in architecture, engineering, and surveying 10,730 (11) $63,600	Occupations in architecture, engineering, and surveying 14,292 (13) $64,756	Occupations in architecture, engineering, and surveying 20,970 (13) $65,000	Occupations in architecture, engineering, and surveying 19,199 (13) $65,000

	Occupations in administrative specializations	Occupations in administrative specializations	Occupations in education	Occupations in administrative specializations	Occupations in education	Occupations in education
10 Of which: #3 occupational group (percent of total) and median earnings	n.a.	6,951 (6) $50,000	8,221 (6) $54,429	7,250 (8) $39,000	9,180 (8) $50,000	14,398 (9) $41,000	16,063 (11) $42,000
11 Of which: Number employed in IT services industry (percent of total)	n.a.	n.a.	60,071 (46)	35,814 (38)	39,323 (35)	51,182 (33)	43,550 (29)
12 Of which: Number employed in IT hardware industry (percent of total)	n.a.	n.a.	4,347 (3)	2,293 (2)	3,774 (3)	6,956 (4)	5,481 (4)

n.a. = not available

a. Period from May 1998 to July 1999.

b. Defined as North American Industry Classification System (NAICS) categories (3341) Computer and Peripheral Equipment and (3344) Semiconductor and Other Electronic Component Manufacturing.

c. Defined as NAICS categories (5415) Computer Systems Design and Related Services, (5141) Information Services, (5142) Data Processing Services, and (5112) Software Publishers. Due to USCIS policy of publishing data for only select industries each year, data for all industries are not available for each year.

d. Actual issuance by the US State Department of H-1B visas in 1996, 1997, and 1998 amounted to 58,327, 80,547, and 91,360, respectively. India, China, and Britain are ranked one, two, and three, respectively, in terms of country nationals issuance from 2000 to 2002.

e. Includes 20,000 H-1Bs reserved for master's degree (or higher) graduates from US universities.

Note: The shaded areas in the table denote H-1B petitions that are exempt from the congressional cap on H-1B visas.

Sources: US Department of State, Bureau of Consular Affairs (2000 to 2006); INS (2000b, 2002a, 2002b); US Department of Homeland Security, Office of Immigration Statistics (2003b, 2004b); USCIS (2006a, 2006b). It must be emphasized that the USCIS caveats these reports on H-1B visas by stating that "very little editing has been done to the data," and there may consequently be some errors in the data. Whether these errors are likely to be systematic cannot be discerned.

Table A.3 Top 200 H-1B employers, 2006

Rank	Company	Sector	Home country	Number of visas
1	Infosys Technologies Ltd.	IT services/software	India	4,908
2	Wipro Ltd.	IT services/software	India	4,002
3	Microsoft Corporation	IT services/software	United States	3,117
4	Tata Consultancy Services Ltd.	IT services/software	India	3,046
5	Satyam Computer Services Ltd.	IT services/software	India	2,880
6	Cognizant Tech Solutions US Corporation	IT services/software	India	2,226
7	Patni Computer Systems, Inc.	IT services/software	India	1,391
8	IBM Corporation	IT services/software	United States	1,130
9	Oracle USA, Inc.	IT services/software	United States	1,022
10	Larsen & Toubro Infotech Ltd.	IT services/software	India	947
11	HCL America, Inc.	IT services/software	India	910
12	Deloitte & Touche LLP	Accounting	United States	890
13	Cisco Systems, Inc.	ICT hardware	United States	828
14	Intel Corporation	Semiconductors	United States	828
15	I-Flex Solutions, Inc.	IT services/software	India	817
16	Ernst & Young LLP	Accounting	United States	774
17	Tech Mahindra Americas, Inc.	IT services/software	India	770
18	Motorola, Inc.	ICT hardware	United States	760
19	Mphasis Corporation	IT services/software	India	751
20	Deloitte Consulting LLP	Consulting	United States	665
21	Lancesoft, Inc.	IT services/software	United States	645
22	New York City Public Schools	Education	United States	642
23	Accenture LLP	Consulting	United States	637
24	JPMorgan Chase & Co.	Financial services	United States	632
25	Polaris Software Lab India Ltd.	IT services/software	India	611
26	Covansys Corporation	IT services/software	United States	611
27	PricewaterhouseCoopers LLP	Accounting	United States	591
28	Qualcomm Incorporated	Telecommunications	United States	533
29	Goldman Sachs & Co.	Financial services	United States	529
30	KPMG LLP	Accounting	United States	476
31	Marlabs, Inc.	IT services/software	United States	475
32	University of Michigan	Education	United States	437
33	University of Illinois at Chicago	Education	United States	434
34	University of Pennsylvania	Education	United States	432
35	The Johns Hopkins University Medical Institutes	Education	United States	432
36	Syntel Consulting, Inc.	IT services/software	United States	416
37	Citigroup Global Markets, Inc.	Financial services	United States	413
38	Bearingpoint, Inc.	Consulting	United States	413
39	University of Maryland	Education	United States	404
40	Keane, Inc.	Consulting	United States	386
41	HTC Global Services, Inc.	IT services/software	United States	382
42	Igate Mastech, Inc.	IT services/software	United States	378

Table A.3 *(continued)*

Rank	Company	Sector	Home country	Number of visas
43	Hexaware Technologies, Inc.	IT services/software	India	362
44	Capital One Services, Inc.	Financial services	United States	362
45	Columbia University	Education	United States	355
46	Lehman Brothers, Inc.	Financial services	United States	352
47	Yahoo, Inc.	IT services/software	United States	347
48	US Technology Resources LLC	IT services/software	United States	339
49	Intelligroup, Inc.	IT services/software	United States	336
50	Hewlett Packard Co.	IT hardware	United States	333
51	Rapidigm, Inc.	IT services/software	United States	330
52	Merrill Lynch & Co., Inc.	Financial services	United States	329
53	Google, Inc.	Internet	United States	328
54	Citibank, N.A.	Financial services	United States	322
55	National Institutes of Health, US Department of Health and Human Services	Medical	United States	322
56	Yale University	Education	United States	316
57	Nokia, Inc.	Telecommunications	Finland	314
58	Texas Instruments, Inc.	IT hardware	United States	313
59	Capgemini US LLC	Consulting	France	309
60	Harvard University	Education	United States	308
61	EMC Corporation	IT services/software	United States	305
62	Sun Microsystems, Inc.	IT services/software	United States	303
63	Rite Aid Corporation	Medical/retail	United States	301
64	Bloomberg	Financial services	United States	298
65	General Electric Company	Manufacturing	United States	292
66	Amgen, Inc.	Medical	United States	289
67	McKinsey & Company, Inc. US	Consulting	United States	286
68	Morgan Stanley	Financial services	United States	285
69	Stanford University	Education	United States	279
70	Washington University in St. Louis	Education	United States	278
71	Verizon Data Services, Inc.	Telecommunications	United States	276
72	NYC Harlem Hospital Center	Medical	United States	276
73	University of Pittsburgh	Education	United States	275
74	Indiana University	Education	United States	273
75	Ohio State University	Education	United States	271
76	Everest Consulting Group, Inc.	IT services/ telecommunications	United States	269
77	University of Minnesota	Education	United States	269
78	Amtex Systems, Inc.	IT services/software	United States	268
79	University of Wisconsin at Madison	Education	United States	268

(table continues next page)

Table A.3 Top 200 H-1B employers, 2006 *(continued)*

Rank	Company	Sector	Home country	Number of visas
80	State University of New York at Stony Brook	Education	United States	262
81	Amazon Global Resources, Inc.	IT services/software	United States	262
82	Cleveland Clinic Foundation	Medical	United States	256
83	Dallas Independent School District	Education	United States	255
84	University of California, Davis	Education	United States	254
85	Northwestern University	Education	United States	251
86	Syntel, Inc.	IT services/software	United States	250
87	University of Missouri, Columbia	Education	United States	247
88	Globalcynex, Inc.	IT services/software	United States	247
89	Kanbay Incorporated	IT services/software	India	246
90	American Solutions, Inc.	IT services/software	United States	242
91	University of Florida International Center	Education	United States	240
92	University of California, Los Angeles	Education	United States	239
93	Duke University Medical Center	Education	United States	238
94	Mount Sinai Medical Center	Education	United States	236
95	Bank of America, N.A.	Financial services	United States	236
96	Software Research Group, Inc.	IT services/software	United States	234
97	Baylor College of Medicine	Education	United States	234
98	Massachusetts General Hospital	Medical	United States	232
99	Ciber, Inc.	IT services/software	United States	232
100	Verinon Technology Solutions Ltd.	IT services/software	India	230
101	Everest Business Solutions, Inc.	IT services/telecomunications	United States	226
102	Volt Technical Resources LLC	IT services/software	United States	224
103	Oklahoma State University	Education	United States	223
104	Compunnel Software Group, Inc.	IT services/software	United States	222
105	US Tech Solutions, Inc.	IT services/software	United States	221
106	Symantec Corporation	IT services/software	United States	220
107	JSMN International, Inc.	IT services/software	United States	218
108	UBS AG	Financial services	Switzerland	216
109	CVS Pharmacy	Medical	United States	213
110	Pennsylvania State University	Education	United States	213
111	University of Washington	Education	United States	213
112	Nortel Networks, Inc.	IT hardware	Canada	212

Table A.3 *(continued)*

Rank	Company	Sector	Home country	Number of visas
113	University of California, San Francisco	Education	United States	211
114	University of Massachusetts Medical School	Education	United States	210
115	Sprint/United Management Company	Telecommunications	United States	209
116	Houston Independent School District	Education	United States	209
117	Purdue University	Education	United States	208
118	Global Consultants, Inc.	IT services/software	United States	207
119	Emory University	Education	United States	207
120	University of Texas Health Science Center	Education	United States	207
121	University of Colorado	Education	United States	207
122	Vanderbilt University	Education	United States	205
123	Objectwin Technology, Inc.	IT services/software	United States	205
124	Diaspark, Inc.	IT services/software	India	204
125	HSBC Bank USA, N.A.	Financial services	United States	203
126	Ebusiness Application Solutions	IT services/software	United States	203
127	Broadcom Corporation	Semiconductors	United States	203
128	Prince Georges County Public Schools	Education	United States	203
129	Micron Technology, Inc.	IT hardware	United States	202
130	Countrywide Home Loans, Inc.	Financial services	United States	198
131	Texas A&M University	Education	United States	198
132	Applied Materials, Inc.	Semiconductors	United States	195
133	Schlumberger Technology Corporation	Oil services	France	194
134	University of Iowa	Education	United States	194
135	IBM Global Services (IGS) India Pvt. Ltd.	IT services/software	United States	194
136	Deloitte Tax LLP	Accounting	United States	194
137	Cummins, Inc.	Manufacturing	United States	193
138	Itech US, Inc.	IT services/software	United States	191
139	Compuware Corporation	IT services/software	United States	189
140	International Students and Scholars Office	Education	United States	186
141	University of California, San Diego	Education	United States	185
142	Walgreen Co.	Medical	United States	184
143	Howard Hughes Medical Institute	Education	United States	184

(table continues next page)

Table A.3 Top 200 H-1B employers, 2006 *(continued)*

Rank	Company	Sector	Home country	Number of visas
144	University of Southern California	Education	United States	183
145	Vision Systems Group, Inc.	IT services/software	United States	182
146	T Mobile USA, Inc.	Telecommunications	Germany	180
147	Multivision, Inc.	Media	United States	178
148	Electronic Data Systems (EDS)	IT services/software	United States	177
149	Massachusetts Institute of Technology	Education	United States	175
150	California Institute of Technology	Education	United States	174
151	Case Western Reserve University	Education	United States	173
152	University of North Carolina, Chapel Hill	Education	United States	173
153	University of Alabama, Birmingham	Education	United States	172
154	Deutsche Bank AG	Financial services	Germany	170
155	Caterpillar, Inc.	Manufacturing	United States	170
156	Hallmark Global Technologies, Inc.	IT services/software	United States	169
157	Cyberthink, Inc.	IT services/software	United States	169
158	Corporate Computer Services, Inc.	IT services/software	United States	167
159	Advanced Micro Devices, Inc.	Semiconductors	United States	167
160	Megasoft Consultants, Inc.	IT services/software	India	166
161	Enterprise Solutions, Inc.	IT services/software	United States	165
162	Freescale Semiconductor, Inc.	Semiconductors	United States	163
163	University of Texas Southwestern Medical Center	Education	United States	163
164	First Tek Technologies, Inc.	IT services/software	United States	161
165	Michigan State University	Education	United States	161
166	Research Foundation of the State University of New York	Education	United States	160
167	Comsys Services LLC	IT services/software	United States	160
168	Virginia Tech	Education	United States	160
169	Juniper Networks, Inc.	ICT hardware	United States	160
170	University of Arizona	Education	United States	158
171	Iowa State University	Education	United States	157
172	University of Virginia	Education	United States	157
173	Fedex Corporate Services, Inc.	Courier services	United States	157
174	Credit Suisse First Boston LLC	Financial services	Switzerland	156
175	Bristol-Myers Squibb Company	Medical	United States	156
176	Verizon Services Corporation	Telecommunications	United States	156

Table A.3 *(continued)*

Rank	Company	Sector	Home country	Number of visas
177	eBay, Inc.	Internet	United States	155
178	Ajilon Consulting	Consulting	France	154
179	General Motors Corporation	Manufacturing	United States	153
180	Camo Technologies, Inc.	IT services/software	United States	152
181	Marvell Semiconductor, Inc.	Semiconductors	United States	151
182	CMC Americas, Inc.	Manufacturing	United States	150
183	University of Texas M. D. Anderson Cancer Center	Education	United States	149
184	Nvidia Corporation	IT hardware	United States	149
185	AT&T Services, Inc.	Telecommunications	United States	147
186	Weill Medical College of Cornell University	Education	United States	146
187	Axiom Systems, Inc.	IT services/software	United Kingdom	146
188	Wayne State University	Education	United States	146
189	Mayo Clinic, Rochester	Education	United States	146
190	North Carolina State University	Education	United States	146
191	Genentech, Inc.	Medical	United States	146
192	Makro Technologies, Inc.	IT services/software	United States	145
193	Svam International, Inc.	IT services/software	United States	144
194	Memorial Sloan-Kettering Cancer Center	Medical	United States	143
195	Nutech Information Systems	IT services/software	United States	143
196	Xpedite Technologies, Inc.	IT services/software	United States	143
197	Automatic Data Processing, Inc.	IT services/software	United States	143
198	Louisiana State University	Education	United States	142
199	Fannie Mae	Financial services	United States	141
200	Mindtree Consulting Pvt. Ltd.	IT services/software	India	141

	Percent share of total visas: 100	Total number of visas: 77,851
IT services/software	53	41,634
Education	19	14,633
Financial services	6	4,842
Other sectors	22	16,742
Indian companies (all IT services/software)	32	24,608
US companies	66	51,408
Other countries	2	1,835

Source: Marianne Kolbasuk McGee, "Who Gets H-1B Visas? Check Out This List," *InformationWeek,* May 17, 2007.

Table A.4 Employment and wage developments in the United States, software workers and other major occupational categories, 1999-2006

Occupational category/ period	Total employment	Annual mean wage	Annual base wages (current dollars) 10th percentile	25th percentile	Median wage	75th percentile	90th percentile
All occupations[a]							
2001Q4	127,980,410	34,020	14,070	18,140	27,060	42,240	62,880
2002Q4	127,523,760	35,560	14,450	18,580	27,690	43,340	64,900
2003Q2	127,567,910	36,210	14,640	18,880	28,140	44,040	66,500
2003Q4	127,420,170	36,520	14,750	19,060	28,400	44,500	67,330
2004Q2	128,127,360	37,020	14,880	19,300	28,770	45,060	68,510
2004Q4	129,146,700	37,440	14,990	19,470	29,070	45,640	69,300
2005Q2	130,307,840	37,870	15,110	19,680	29,430	46,180	70,180
2006Q2	132,604,980	39,190	15,500	20,270	30,400	47,820	72,960
Computer and mathematical							
1999Q4	2,620,080	54,930	29,340	38,700	51,990	68,250	86,380
2000Q4	2,932,810	58,050	30,190	40,560	55,110	72,670	90,810
2001Q4	2,825,870	60,350	31,090	42,140	57,650	76,240	94,890
2002Q4	2,772,620	61,630	31,730	42,930	58,500	77,220	95,690
2003Q2	2,827,010	63,240	32,460	44,020	60,060	79,390	98,000
2003Q4	2,830,550	64,150	33,010	44,740	61,100	80,630	99,810
2004Q2	2,915,300	65,510	33,780	45,820	62,620	82,540	102,930
2004Q4	2,932,790	66,370	34,380	46,500	63,440	83,540	104,280
2005Q2	2,952,740	67,100	34,460	46,730	63,940	84,520	106,090
2006Q2	3,076,200	69,240	35,490	48,090	66,130	87,310	109,240
Computer programmers							
1999Q4	528,600	54,960	29,650	38,780	51,060	72,780	91,260
2000Q4	530,730	60,970	35,020	44,850	57,590	74,500	93,210
2001Q4	501,550	62,890	35,390	46,160	60,110	77,830	96,390
2002Q4	457,320	63,690	35,080	45,960	60,290	78,140	96,860
2003Q2	431,640	64,510	35,560	46,640	61,340	79,210	97,000
2003Q4	403,220	65,170	35,870	46,860	61,730	79,780	97,910
2004Q2	412,090	65,910	36,470	47,580	62,890	81,280	99,610
2004Q4	396,100	66,480	37,170	47,870	62,980	81,730	100,980
2005Q2	389,090	67,400	37,380	48,040	63,420	82,600	103,850
2006Q2	396,020	69,500	38,460	49,580	65,510	85,080	106,610
Computer software engineers, applications							
1999Q4	287,600	65,780	39,800	49,880	63,330	80,210	98,980
2000Q4	374,640	70,300	42,710	53,390	67,670	85,490	106,680
2001Q4	361,690	72,370	44,380	55,210	70,210	88,060	109,170
2002Q4	356,760	73,800	44,830	55,510	70,900	88,660	109,800
2003Q2	392,140	75,750	45,970	56,930	72,530	89,940	111,860
2003Q4	410,580	76,260	45,480	57,570	73,410	90,830	112,940
2004Q2	425,890	77,330	46,520	59,130	74,980	92,130	113,830
2004Q4	439,720	78,570	47,340	60,220	76,310	93,560	114,690
2005Q2	455,980	79,540	47,370	60,420	77,090	94,970	116,150
2006Q2	472,520	82,000	49,350	62,830	79,780	98,470	119,770

Employment and real base wage index (1999Q4 = 100, CPI deflated)

Total employment	Annual mean wage	10th percentile	25th percentile	Median wage	75th percentile	90th percentile
100	100.0	100.0	100.0	100.0	100.0	100.0
100	102.2	100.4	100.2	100.1	100.3	100.9
100	103.1	100.8	100.8	100.7	101.0	102.4
100	103.0	100.6	100.8	100.7	101.1	102.8
100	102.5	99.6	100.2	100.1	100.5	102.6
101	102.2	98.9	99.7	99.8	100.3	102.3
102	101.9	98.3	99.3	99.5	100.0	102.1
104	101.4	96.9	98.3	98.9	99.6	102.1
100	100.0	100.0	100.0	100.0	100.0	100.0
112	102.2	99.5	101.3	102.5	102.9	101.6
108	104.3	100.6	103.3	105.2	106.0	104.2
106	104.1	100.4	102.9	104.4	105.0	102.8
108	105.8	101.7	104.5	106.2	106.9	104.3
108	106.4	102.5	105.3	107.0	107.6	105.2
111	106.6	102.9	105.8	107.6	108.1	106.5
112	106.5	103.3	105.9	107.5	107.9	106.4
113	106.1	102.0	104.9	106.8	107.5	106.7
117	105.3	101.0	103.8	106.2	106.8	105.6
100	100.0	100.0	100.0	100.0	100.0	100.0
100	107.2	114.2	111.8	109.0	99.0	98.7
95	108.6	113.3	113.0	111.7	101.5	100.2
87	107.5	109.8	110.0	109.6	99.6	98.5
82	107.9	110.2	110.5	110.4	100.0	97.7
76	108.0	110.2	110.1	110.1	99.8	97.7
78	107.2	109.9	109.7	110.1	99.8	97.5
75	106.6	110.5	108.8	108.7	99.0	97.5
74	106.5	109.5	107.6	107.9	98.6	98.8
75	105.6	108.3	106.8	107.1	97.6	97.6
100	100.0	100.0	100.0	100.0	100.0	100.0
130	103.3	103.7	103.5	103.3	103.0	104.2
126	104.4	105.8	105.0	105.2	104.2	104.7
124	104.1	104.5	103.3	103.9	102.6	102.9
136	105.8	106.1	104.9	105.2	103.0	103.8
143	105.6	104.1	105.1	105.6	103.1	103.9
148	105.1	104.5	105.9	105.8	102.7	102.8
153	105.3	104.8	106.4	106.2	102.8	102.1
159	105.0	103.4	105.2	105.7	102.8	101.9
164	104.1	103.5	105.2	105.2	102.5	101.0

(table continues next page)

Table A.4 Employment and wage developments in the United States, software workers and other major occupational categories, 1999-2006 *(continued)*

Occupational category/ period	Total employment	Annual mean wage	10th percentile	25th percentile	Median wage	75th percentile	90th percentile
Computer software engineers, systems software							
1999Q4	209,030	66,230	40,360	50,590	64,620	81,260	96,990
2000Q4	264,610	70,890	43,600	54,460	69,530	86,520	105,240
2001Q4	261,520	74,490	45,820	57,700	73,280	90,450	110,750
2002Q4	255,040	75,840	45,980	58,500	74,040	91,160	111,600
2003Q2	285,760	78,400	47,870	60,460	76,240	93,190	114,070
2003Q4	292,520	79,790	48,960	61,300	77,250	95,080	116,020
2004Q2	318,020	82,160	50,420	63,150	79,740	98,220	118,350
2004Q4	321,120	83,460	51,380	64,300	81,140	100,370	119,750
2005Q2	320,720	84,310	51,890	65,070	82,120	101,780	120,410
2006Q2	329,060	87,250	53,580	67,620	85,370	105,330	125,750
Management							
1999Q4	8,063,410	64,740	27,830	39,340	57,580	84,180	123,140
2000Q4	7,782,680	68,190	29,220	41,500	61,310	89,020	132,710
2001Q4	7,212,360	70,800	30,410	43,340	64,220	93,120	138,570
2002Q4	7,092,460	78,870	31,850	45,470	67,120	97,320	144,620
2003Q2	6,653,480	82,790	33,590	48,140	70,870	102,730	n.a.
2003Q4	6,439,530	83,400	34,380	49,160	72,180	104,670	n.a.
2004Q2	6,200,940	85,530	35,760	50,890	74,390	107,900	n.a.
2004Q4	6,085,780	87,090	36,800	52,120	75,960	109,730	n.a.
2005Q2	5,960,560	88,450	37,800	53,400	77,630	111,750	n.a.
2006Q2	5,892,900	91,930	39,380	55,820	80,980	116,240	n.a.
Business and financial operations							
1999Q4	4,361,980	46,100	24,170	31,360	41,770	55,560	72,860
2000Q4	4,619,270	48,470	25,340	32,950	43,900	58,640	78,450
2001Q4	4,676,680	50,580	26,320	34,260	45,720	61,700	82,650
2002Q4	4,772,120	53,350	27,290	35,470	47,350	64,020	85,890
2003Q2	4,924,210	55,550	28,420	36,860	49,260	66,760	89,000
2003Q4	5,045,860	56,000	28,600	37,130	49,740	67,470	89,880
2004Q2	5,131,840	56,380	29,000	37,630	50,350	68,160	90,100
2004Q4	5,253,720	57,120	29,440	38,130	51,000	68,970	90,850
2005Q2	5,410,410	57,930	29,780	38,660	51,760	69,940	92,110
2006Q2	5,826,140	60,000	30,620	39,860	53,690	72,650	95,890
Architecture and engineering							
1999Q4	2,506,380	51,600	27,290	36,470	49,220	64,860	81,820
2000Q4	2,575,620	54,060	28,630	38,050	51,530	67,960	85,960
2001Q4	2,489,070	56,330	29,860	39,710	53,630	70,650	88,950
2002Q4	2,411,260	58,020	30,370	40,600	54,900	72,530	90,750
2003Q2	2,376,650	59,230	30,870	41,360	55,930	73,980	92,040
2003Q4	2,354,580	60,390	31,480	42,220	56,940	75,600	93,680
2004Q2	2,372,770	61,750	32,090	43,140	58,120	77,450	95,980
2004Q4	2,385,680	63,060	32,840	44,190	59,410	79,350	98,790
2005Q2	2,382,480	63,910	33,160	44,760	60,200	80,470	100,880
2006Q2	2,430,250	66,190	33,970	45,960	62,390	83,250	104,250

Header row (spanning): Annual base wages (current dollars)

Employment and real base wage index (1999Q4 = 100, CPI deflated)

Total employment	Annual mean wage	10th percentile	25th percentile	Median wage	75th percentile	90th percentile
100	100.0	100.0	100.0	100.0	100.0	100.0
127	103.5	104.4	104.1	104.0	102.9	104.9
125	106.7	107.7	108.2	107.6	105.6	108.4
122	106.3	105.7	107.3	106.3	104.1	106.8
137	108.8	109.0	109.8	108.4	105.4	108.1
140	109.7	110.5	110.4	108.9	106.6	108.9
152	110.9	111.6	111.6	110.3	108.0	109.1
154	111.0	112.2	112.0	110.7	108.8	108.8
153	110.5	111.6	111.7	110.4	108.8	107.8
157	110.0	110.9	111.6	110.3	108.2	108.3
100	100.0	100.0	100.0	100.0	100.0	100.0
97	101.8	101.5	102.0	102.9	102.2	104.2
89	103.8	103.7	104.5	105.8	105.0	106.8
88	113.1	106.2	107.3	108.2	107.3	109.0
83	117.5	110.9	112.4	113.1	112.1	n.a.
80	117.3	112.5	113.8	114.2	113.2	n.a.
77	118.1	114.8	115.6	115.5	114.6	n.a.
75	118.5	116.5	116.8	116.3	114.9	n.a.
74	118.6	117.9	117.9	117.1	115.3	n.a.
73	118.6	118.2	118.5	117.4	115.3	n.a.
100	100.0	100.0	100.0	100.0	100.0	100.0
106	101.6	101.4	101.6	101.6	102.0	104.1
107	104.1	103.3	103.7	103.9	105.4	107.6
109	107.4	104.8	105.0	105.2	106.9	109.4
113	110.7	108.0	108.0	108.4	110.4	112.2
116	110.6	107.8	107.8	108.5	110.6	112.4
118	109.3	107.2	107.2	107.7	109.6	110.5
120	109.2	107.3	107.1	107.6	109.4	109.9
124	109.1	107.0	107.1	107.6	109.3	109.8
134	108.7	105.8	106.1	107.3	109.2	109.9
100	100.0	100.0	100.0	100.0	100.0	100.0
103	101.3	101.4	100.9	101.2	101.3	101.6
99	103.6	103.8	103.3	103.4	103.4	103.2
96	104.3	103.3	103.3	103.5	103.8	102.9
95	105.5	103.9	104.2	104.4	104.8	103.4
94	106.6	105.1	105.4	105.4	106.2	104.3
95	106.9	105.1	105.7	105.5	106.7	104.8
95	107.7	106.0	106.8	106.4	107.8	106.4
95	107.6	105.5	106.6	106.2	107.7	107.1
97	107.1	103.9	105.2	105.9	107.2	106.4

(table continues next page)

Table A.4 Employment and wage developments in the United States, software workers and other major occupational categories, 1999-2006 *(continued)*

Occupational category/ period	Total employment	Annual mean wage	Annual base wages (current dollars)				
			10th percentile	25th percentile	Median wage	75th percentile	90th percentile
Life, physical, and social sciences							
1999Q4	909,530	45,660	22,600	30,180	41,600	56,200	75,130
2000Q4	1,038,670	47,790	23,150	31,130	43,090	59,310	81,360
2001Q4	1,067,730	49,710	24,000	32,280	44,770	62,340	84,670
2002Q4	1,078,630	52,380	24,790	33,340	46,370	64,920	88,260
2003Q2	1,113,130	53,210	24,850	33,460	46,970	66,580	89,650
2003Q4	1,102,070	54,930	26,130	34,980	48,660	68,450	91,790
2004Q2	1,131,390	55,920	26,270	35,380	49,670	70,170	94,160
2004Q4	1,144,240	57,550	28,060	36,870	51,150	71,560	96,550
2005Q2	1,185,730	58,030	27,690	36,840	51,540	72,320	98,450
2006Q2	1,231,070	59,660	28,490	37,830	53,010	74,730	101,110
Community and social services							
1999Q4	1,404,540	31,640	17,000	21,970	29,130	39,290	50,660
2000Q4	1,469,000	32,910	17,710	22,800	30,240	40,830	52,700
2001Q4	1,523,890	34,190	18,370	23,660	31,440	42,330	54,660
2002Q4	1,576,980	34,630	18,590	23,900	31,690	42,830	55,410
2003Q2	1,615,610	35,420	19,010	24,450	32,400	43,660	56,450
2003Q4	1,654,420	35,800	19,140	24,720	32,880	44,150	56,970
2004Q2	1,673,740	36,440	19,470	25,130	33,460	44,840	57,800
2004Q4	1,680,750	37,050	19,910	25,660	33,940	45,540	58,560
2005Q2	1,692,950	37,530	20,170	25,970	34,360	46,080	59,310
2006Q2	1,749,210	39,000	20,770	26,850	35,790	48,270	62,280
Legal							
1999Q4	858,320	66,780	25,140	34,080	55,120	97,020	141,920
2000Q4	890,910	68,930	26,230	35,790	56,880	99,790	n.a.
2001Q4	909,370	69,030	26,550	36,120	56,220	99,370	n.a.
2002Q4	934,850	77,330	27,410	37,480	58,010	101,720	n.a.
2003Q2	951,510	78,910	28,180	38,270	59,200	103,720	n.a.
2003Q4	945,440	78,590	28,700	38,620	59,400	104,380	n.a.
2004Q2	958,520	79,910	29,370	39,530	60,820	106,680	n.a.
2004Q4	973,970	81,180	29,810	40,360	62,400	108,660	n.a.
2005Q2	986,740	81,070	30,040	40,840	62,890	109,260	n.a.
2006Q2	976,740	85,360	31,290	42,960	67,730	116,170	n.a.
Education, training, and library							
1999Q4	7,344,830	36,040	14,580	22,230	33,580	45,860	60,450
2000Q4	7,450,860	37,900	15,420	23,070	34,900	48,570	64,670
2001Q4	7,658,480	39,130	15,970	23,840	36,210	50,220	66,430
2002Q4	7,772,470	40,160	16,320	24,420	36,940	51,310	67,760
2003Q2	7,831,630	40,660	16,660	24,830	37,430	52,020	68,590
2003Q4	7,852,030	41,390	16,960	25,230	37,980	52,780	69,640
2004Q2	7,891,810	42,080	17,320	25,700	38,620	53,550	70,500
2004Q4	7,969,800	42,810	17,710	26,120	39,170	54,250	71,520
2005Q2	8,078,500	43,450	18,030	26,490	39,600	54,940	72,670
2006Q2	8,206,440	45,320	18,690	27,550	41,100	57,060	75,970

Employment and real base wage index (1999Q4 = 100, CPI deflated)

Total employment	Annual mean wage	10th percentile	25th percentile	Median wage	75th percentile	90th percentile
100	100.0	100.0	100.0	100.0	100.0	100.0
114	101.2	99.0	99.7	100.1	102.0	104.7
117	103.3	100.8	101.5	102.1	105.3	106.9
119	106.5	101.8	102.5	103.4	107.2	109.0
122	107.1	101.0	101.9	103.8	108.9	109.6
121	109.6	105.3	105.6	106.5	110.9	111.3
124	109.5	103.9	104.8	106.7	111.6	112.0
126	111.1	109.4	107.7	108.4	112.2	113.2
130	110.4	106.4	106.0	107.6	111.7	113.8
135	109.1	105.3	104.7	106.4	111.0	112.4
100	100.0	100.0	100.0	100.0	100.0	100.0
105	100.6	100.7	100.3	100.4	100.5	100.6
108	102.5	102.5	102.2	102.4	102.2	102.4
112	101.6	101.5	101.0	101.0	101.2	101.5
115	102.9	102.8	102.3	102.2	102.1	102.4
118	103.1	102.5	102.5	102.8	102.3	102.4
119	102.9	102.4	102.2	102.7	102.0	102.0
120	103.2	103.2	102.9	102.7	102.1	101.9
121	103.0	103.0	102.6	102.4	101.8	101.7
125	102.9	102.0	102.1	102.6	102.6	102.7
100	100.0	100.0	100.0	100.0	100.0	100.0
104	99.8	100.9	101.5	99.8	99.4	n.a.
106	98.1	100.2	100.6	96.8	97.2	n.a.
109	107.5	101.2	102.1	97.7	97.3	n.a.
111	108.6	103.0	103.2	98.7	98.2	n.a.
110	107.2	104.0	103.2	98.1	98.0	n.a.
112	106.9	104.4	103.7	98.6	98.3	n.a.
113	107.1	104.5	104.4	99.8	98.7	n.a.
115	105.4	103.8	104.1	99.1	97.8	n.a.
114	106.7	103.9	105.3	102.6	100.0	n.a.
100	100.0	100.0	100.0	100.0	100.0	100.0
101	101.7	102.2	100.3	100.5	102.4	103.4
104	103.0	103.9	101.8	102.3	103.9	104.3
106	103.4	103.9	101.9	102.1	103.8	104.0
107	103.7	105.0	102.6	102.4	104.2	104.3
107	104.6	105.9	103.4	103.0	104.8	104.9
107	104.3	106.2	103.3	102.8	104.4	104.2
109	104.7	107.0	103.5	102.8	104.2	104.3
110	104.7	107.4	103.5	102.4	104.0	104.4
112	105.0	107.0	103.5	102.2	103.9	104.9

(table continues next page)

Table A.4 Employment and wage developments in the United States, software workers and other major occupational categories, 1999-2006 *(continued)*

Occupational category/ period	Total employment	Annual mean wage	10th percentile	25th percentile	Median wage	75th percentile	90th percentile
Arts, design, entertainment, sports, and media							
1999Q4	1,551,600	37,650	13,920	20,540	31,640	47,980	70,030
2000Q4	1,513,420	38,640	14,780	21,320	32,770	49,330	70,210
2001Q4	1,508,790	39,770	15,110	21,880	33,670	50,210	71,450
2002Q4	1,503,680	41,660	15,810	22,700	34,580	51,680	73,390
2003Q2	1,538,150	42,620	16,000	23,070	35,100	52,680	75,200
2003Q4	1,583,250	43,350	16,460	23,710	35,770	53,090	76,290
2004Q2	1,595,710	43,710	16,590	23,860	36,170	53,840	77,470
2004Q4	1,645,870	43,820	16,680	24,070	36,400	54,090	78,180
2005Q2	1,683,310	44,310	17,050	24,500	36,830	54,810	79,840
2006Q2	1,727,380	46,110	17,620	25,560	38,340	57,040	82,330
Healthcare practitioners and technical							
1999Q4	6,001,950	45,250	20,650	28,510	38,950	52,680	74,300
2000Q4	6,041,210	47,990	21,940	30,060	41,080	55,220	82,950
2001Q4	6,118,970	49,930	22,810	31,300	42,770	57,520	87,090
2002Q4	6,185,020	53,990	23,290	32,040	43,820	58,990	88,760
2003Q2	6,173,760	55,380	23,910	32,980	44,990	60,820	90,990
2003Q4	6,258,560	56,240	24,440	33,770	46,060	62,940	92,910
2004Q2	6,359,380	57,310	24,860	34,540	47,240	64,980	95,220
2004Q4	6,469,920	58,310	25,270	35,290	48,470	66,640	98,100
2005Q2	6,547,350	59,170	25,670	35,980	49,570	68,000	101,140
2006Q2	6,713,780	62,030	26,800	37,420	51,980	71,460	105,970
Healthcare support							
1999Q4	2,970,780	19,780	13,040	15,310	18,560	22,940	28,110
2000Q4	3,039,430	21,040	13,870	16,150	19,760	24,690	30,860
2001Q4	3,122,870	21,900	14,360	16,760	20,490	25,630	32,190
2002Q4	3,173,400	22,410	14,790	17,250	21,040	26,280	32,750
2003Q2	3,208,770	22,750	14,990	17,590	21,360	26,710	33,260
2003Q4	3,235,840	22,960	15,060	17,770	21,530	26,930	33,510
2004Q2	3,271,350	23,220	15,160	18,000	21,730	27,180	33,860
2004Q4	3,307,150	23,510	15,300	18,230	21,950	27,440	34,170
2005Q2	3,363,800	23,850	15,460	18,430	22,140	27,740	34,580
2006Q2	3,483,270	24,610	16,030	18,930	22,870	28,630	35,750
Protective services							
1999Q4	2,958,730	29,650	13,890	17,260	25,810	39,120	52,270
2000Q4	3,009,070	30,780	14,260	17,750	26,660	40,810	54,440
2001Q4	2,957,990	32,530	14,900	19,010	28,410	42,800	56,820
2002Q4	2,993,490	33,330	15,280	19,700	28,850	43,860	58,260
2003Q2	2,999,630	34,090	15,540	20,170	29,650	44,840	59,610
2003Q4	2,983,230	34,430	15,680	20,400	29,900	45,190	60,580
2004Q2	3,006,100	34,840	15,890	20,620	30,300	45,670	61,380
2004Q4	3,059,090	35,240	16,020	20,860	30,790	46,310	62,010
2005Q2	3,056,660	35,750	16,190	21,030	31,200	47,000	63,150
2006Q2	3,024,840	37,040	16,700	21,620	32,070	48,780	65,130

Employment and real base wage index (1999Q4 = 100, CPI deflated)

Total employment	Annual mean wage	10th percentile	25th percentile	Median wage	75th percentile	90th percentile
100	100.0	100.0	100.0	100.0	100.0	100.0
98	99.2	102.6	100.3	100.1	99.4	96.9
97	100.2	103.0	101.1	101.0	99.3	96.8
97	102.7	105.4	102.6	101.4	100.0	97.3
99	104.0	105.6	103.2	101.9	100.9	98.7
102	104.9	107.7	105.1	103.0	100.8	99.2
103	103.8	106.5	103.8	102.2	100.3	98.9
106	102.6	105.6	103.3	101.4	99.3	98.4
108	102.2	106.4	103.6	101.1	99.2	99.0
111	102.3	105.7	103.9	101.2	99.3	98.2
100	100.0	100.0	100.0	100.0	100.0	100.0
101	102.5	102.7	101.9	102.0	101.3	107.9
102	104.7	104.8	104.2	104.2	103.6	111.2
103	110.7	104.7	104.3	104.4	103.9	110.9
103	112.5	106.4	106.3	106.1	106.1	112.5
104	113.2	107.8	107.9	107.7	108.8	113.9
106	113.2	107.6	108.3	108.4	110.2	114.5
108	113.6	107.8	109.1	109.7	111.5	116.4
109	113.5	107.9	109.6	110.5	112.1	118.2
112	114.5	108.4	109.6	111.4	113.3	119.1
100	100.0	100.0	100.0	100.0	100.0	100.0
102	102.8	102.8	102.0	102.9	104.0	106.1
105	105.1	104.5	103.9	104.8	106.0	108.7
107	105.1	105.3	104.6	105.2	106.3	108.1
108	105.7	105.6	105.6	105.8	107.0	108.7
109	105.7	105.2	105.7	105.7	106.9	108.6
110	104.9	103.9	105.1	104.6	105.9	107.7
111	104.7	103.4	104.9	104.2	105.4	107.1
113	104.7	103.0	104.5	103.6	105.0	106.8
117	103.9	102.7	103.3	102.9	104.2	106.2
100	100.0	100.0	100.0	100.0	100.0	100.0
102	100.4	99.2	99.4	99.9	100.8	100.7
100	104.1	101.8	104.5	104.5	103.8	103.2
101	104.3	102.1	105.9	103.7	104.0	103.4
101	105.6	102.8	107.4	105.6	105.3	104.8
101	105.8	102.8	107.6	105.5	105.2	105.6
102	105.0	102.2	106.8	104.9	104.3	104.9
103	104.7	101.6	106.5	105.1	104.3	104.5
103	104.7	101.2	105.8	105.0	104.3	104.9
102	104.3	100.4	104.6	103.8	104.1	104.1

(table continues next page)

Table A.4 Employment and wage developments in the United States, software workers and other major occupational categories, 1999-2006 *(continued)*

Occupational category/ period	Total employment	Annual mean wage	Annual base wages (current dollars)				
			10th percentile	25th percentile	Median wage	75th percentile	90th percentile
Food preparation and serving related							
1999Q4	9,687,970	15,600	11,440	12,400	13,820	17,300	22,150
2000Q4	9,955,060	16,070	11,620	12,660	14,170	17,640	22,940
2001Q4	9,917,660	16,720	11,880	13,080	14,820	18,420	24,110
2002Q4	10,067,080	17,180	12,110	13,370	15,240	19,020	24,900
2003Q2	10,216,620	17,290	12,000	13,310	15,390	19,250	25,370
2003Q4	10,314,820	17,400	12,010	13,350	15,590	19,490	25,630
2004Q2	10,507,390	17,530	11,960	13,330	15,770	19,780	26,020
2004Q4	10,637,260	17,620	11,970	13,360	15,900	19,970	26,240
2005Q2	10,797,700	17,840	12,130	13,590	16,070	20,230	26,560
2006Q2	11,029,280	18,430	12,430	14,060	16,430	20,850	27,510
Building and grounds cleaning and maintenance							
1999Q4	4,274,200	18,910	12,040	13,680	16,810	21,970	29,350
2000Q4	4,318,070	19,570	12,400	14,250	17,380	22,680	30,250
2001Q4	4,275,340	20,380	12,840	14,840	18,120	23,690	31,600
2002Q4	4,262,880	20,850	13,120	15,190	18,570	24,260	32,310
2003Q2	4,260,380	21,060	13,150	15,350	18,770	24,600	32,760
2003Q4	4,274,480	21,290	13,230	15,510	19,060	24,970	33,160
2004Q2	4,300,440	21,490	13,280	15,640	19,290	25,320	33,550
2004Q4	4,323,430	21,670	13,400	15,790	19,540	25,550	33,700
2005Q2	4,342,550	21,930	13,700	15,940	19,760	25,870	34,120
2006Q2	4,396,250	22,580	14,140	16,430	20,290	26,560	34,990
Personal care and services							
1999Q4	2,556,920	20,300	11,840	13,250	16,270	21,990	33,980
2000Q4	2,700,510	20,510	12,070	13,590	16,710	22,350	34,220
2001Q4	2,802,050	21,010	12,410	14,060	17,230	22,950	34,950
2002Q4	2,919,280	21,370	12,610	14,370	17,540	23,390	35,140
2003Q2	2,988,590	21,380	12,540	14,440	17,640	23,420	35,000
2003Q4	3,040,060	21,570	12,570	14,590	17,860	23,770	35,140
2004Q2	3,099,550	21,800	12,590	14,730	18,050	24,030	35,360
2004Q4	3,154,670	22,080	12,630	14,860	18,280	24,550	35,600
2005Q2	3,188,850	22,180	12,920	15,020	18,490	24,720	35,580
2006Q2	3,249,760	22,920	13,290	15,410	19,070	25,510	36,940
Sales and related							
1999Q4	12,938,130	27,060	12,120	13,900	18,750	31,870	52,930
2000Q4	13,506,880	27,990	12,460	14,450	19,410	32,900	54,840
2001Q4	13,418,240	28,920	12,790	14,890	20,040	34,010	56,590
2002Q4	13,339,570	30,610	13,150	15,370	20,770	35,300	58,820
2003Q2	13,534,180	31,250	13,270	15,700	21,210	36,090	60,290
2003Q4	13,522,460	31,560	13,390	15,900	21,480	36,540	61,220
2004Q2	13,507,840	32,210	13,540	16,170	21,860	37,380	63,010
2004Q4	13,713,710	32,280	13,520	16,160	21,860	37,650	63,520
2005Q2	13,930,320	32,800	13,770	16,310	22,140	38,440	64,980
2006Q2	14,114,860	34,350	14,300	16,930	23,160	40,220	68,450

Total employment	Annual mean wage	10th percentile	25th percentile	Median wage	75th percentile	90th percentile
	Employment and real base wage index (1999Q4 = 100, CPI deflated)					
100	100.0	100.0	100.0	100.0	100.0	100.0
103	99.6	98.2	98.7	99.1	98.6	100.1
102	101.7	98.5	100.1	101.8	101.0	103.3
104	102.2	98.2	100.1	102.3	102.0	104.3
105	101.8	96.4	98.6	102.3	102.2	105.2
106	101.6	95.6	98.1	102.7	102.6	105.4
108	100.4	93.4	96.1	102.0	102.2	105.0
110	99.5	92.2	94.9	101.4	101.7	104.4
111	99.3	92.1	95.2	101.0	101.5	104.1
114	98.7	90.7	94.7	99.3	100.6	103.7
100	100.0	100.0	100.0	100.0	100.0	100.0
101	100.0	99.6	100.7	99.9	99.8	99.6
100	102.3	101.2	102.9	102.3	102.3	102.2
100	102.3	101.1	103.0	102.5	102.5	102.2
100	102.3	100.4	103.1	102.6	102.9	102.6
100	102.5	100.1	103.3	103.3	103.5	102.9
101	101.6	98.6	102.2	102.6	103.0	102.2
101	101.0	98.1	101.7	102.4	102.5	101.2
102	100.7	98.8	101.2	102.1	102.3	100.9
103	99.7	98.1	100.3	100.8	101.0	99.6
100	100.0	100.0	100.0	100.0	100.0	100.0
106	97.7	98.5	99.2	99.3	98.3	97.4
110	98.2	99.5	100.7	100.5	99.0	97.6
114	97.7	98.8	100.6	100.0	98.7	96.0
117	96.8	97.3	100.1	99.6	97.9	94.6
119	96.8	96.7	100.3	100.0	98.5	94.2
121	96.0	95.0	99.4	99.1	97.7	93.0
123	95.9	94.0	98.8	99.0	98.4	92.3
125	94.9	94.8	98.4	98.7	97.6	90.9
127	94.3	93.7	97.1	97.9	96.9	90.8
100	100.0	100.0	100.0	100.0	100.0	100.0
104	100.0	99.4	100.5	100.1	99.8	100.2
104	101.4	100.1	101.7	101.4	101.3	101.5
103	105.0	100.7	102.6	102.8	102.8	103.1
105	106.1	100.6	103.8	103.9	104.1	104.7
105	106.2	100.6	104.2	104.3	104.4	105.3
104	106.4	99.8	104.0	104.2	104.8	106.4
106	105.1	98.3	102.5	102.7	104.1	105.8
108	105.3	98.7	101.9	102.5	104.7	106.6
109	106.0	98.5	101.7	103.1	105.4	108.0

(table continues next page)

Table A.4   Employment and wage developments in the United States, software workers and other major occupational categories, 1999-2006 *(continued)*

Occupational category/ period	Total employment	Annual mean wage	Annual base wages (current dollars)				
			10th percentile	25th percentile	Median wage	75th percentile	90th percentile
Office and administrative support							
1999Q4	22,562,480	25,310	14,560	18,060	23,160	30,630	39,550
2000Q4	22,936,140	26,300	15,010	18,720	24,140	31,980	41,020
2001Q4	22,798,590	27,230	15,530	19,390	25,050	33,140	42,240
2002Q4	22,754,570	27,910	15,900	19,880	25,670	33,970	43,070
2003Q2	22,678,010	28,260	16,020	20,100	26,040	34,450	43,520
2003Q4	22,607,360	28,540	16,130	20,230	26,240	34,670	44,210
2004Q2	22,649,080	29,020	16,390	20,570	26,710	35,200	44,750
2004Q4	22,622,500	29,390	16,530	20,720	26,960	35,520	45,690
2005Q2	22,784,330	29,710	16,640	20,870	27,240	35,860	46,140
2006Q2	23,077,190	30,370	17,040	21,480	28,080	36,920	46,960
Farming, fishing, and forestry							
1999Q4	463,360	18,000	12,130	12,900	14,480	20,270	29,680
2000Q4	460,700	18,860	12,430	13,320	15,260	21,360	31,060
2001Q4	453,050	19,630	13,030	13,890	16,140	22,090	32,110
2002Q4	451,140	20,220	13,370	14,500	16,660	22,590	32,740
2003Q2	461,630	20,200	13,190	14,620	16,910	22,670	32,420
2003Q4	460,820	20,290	13,330	14,770	17,040	22,810	32,370
2004Q2	458,850	20,310	13,270	14,900	17,110	22,630	32,500
2004Q4	444,870	20,670	13,520	15,200	17,350	23,160	33,250
2005Q2	443,070	21,010	13,850	15,410	17,490	23,580	33,860
2006Q2	450,040	21,810	14,330	15,520	17,950	24,710	35,780
Construction and extraction							
1999Q4	5,938,860	33,650	17,380	22,220	30,820	42,740	54,780
2000Q4	6,187,360	34,440	17,850	22,790	31,490	43,630	56,110
2001Q4	6,239,430	35,450	18,390	23,490	32,390	44,850	58,010
2002Q4	6,124,600	36,340	18,750	24,030	33,160	45,960	59,500
2003Q2	6,085,510	36,650	18,940	24,230	33,360	46,260	60,150
2003Q4	6,099,360	37,000	19,110	24,460	33,710	46,780	60,660
2004Q2	6,170,410	37,520	19,370	24,810	34,060	47,290	61,940
2004Q4	6,303,180	37,890	19,550	25,070	34,330	47,750	62,540
2005Q2	6,370,400	38,260	19,770	25,340	34,650	48,090	63,180
2006Q2	6,680,710	39,290	20,480	26,140	35,450	49,290	64,800
Installation, maintenance, and repair							
1999Q4	5,140,210	32,810	17,310	22,630	30,870	41,170	51,900
2000Q4	5,318,490	33,760	17,790	23,230	31,940	42,490	53,380
2001Q4	5,323,070	34,960	18,410	24,080	33,110	43,960	55,000
2002Q4	5,215,970	35,780	18,750	24,620	33,830	45,020	56,180
2003Q2	5,226,080	36,210	18,950	24,950	34,290	45,490	56,610
2003Q4	5,207,650	36,560	19,090	25,200	34,550	45,820	57,010
2004Q2	5,215,390	37,220	19,480	25,740	35,180	46,460	57,660
2004Q4	5,246,720	37,620	19,660	26,000	35,520	47,010	58,250
2005Q2	5,305,260	38,050	19,840	26,260	35,870	47,550	58,950
2006Q2	5,352,420	39,060	20,490	26,970	36,720	48,970	61,240

Total employment	Annual mean wage	10th percentile	25th percentile	Median wage	75th percentile	90th percentile
100	100.0	100.0	100.0	100.0	100.0	100.0
102	100.5	99.7	100.2	100.8	100.9	100.3
101	102.1	101.2	101.9	102.6	102.7	101.3
101	102.3	101.3	102.2	102.9	102.9	101.1
101	102.6	101.1	102.3	103.3	103.3	101.1
100	102.7	100.9	102.0	103.2	103.1	101.8
100	102.5	100.6	101.8	103.1	102.7	101.1
100	102.3	100.0	101.1	102.6	102.2	101.8
101	101.9	99.2	100.3	102.1	101.7	101.3
102	100.2	97.7	99.3	101.2	100.7	99.2
100	100.0	100.0	100.0	100.0	100.0	100.0
99	101.3	99.1	99.8	101.9	101.9	101.2
98	103.5	101.9	102.2	105.8	103.4	102.7
97	104.2	102.3	104.3	106.8	103.4	102.4
100	103.1	99.9	104.1	107.3	102.8	100.4
99	102.7	100.1	104.3	107.2	102.5	99.3
99	100.8	97.8	103.2	105.6	99.8	97.9
96	101.2	98.2	103.8	105.6	100.7	98.7
96	101.4	99.1	103.7	104.9	101.0	99.1
97	101.2	98.7	100.5	103.5	101.8	100.7
100	100.0	100.0	100.0	100.0	100.0	100.0
104	98.9	99.3	99.2	98.8	98.7	99.0
105	100.0	100.4	100.3	99.7	99.6	100.5
103	100.2	100.1	100.4	99.8	99.8	100.8
102	100.1	100.1	100.2	99.5	99.5	100.9
103	100.1	100.1	100.3	99.6	99.7	100.9
104	99.6	99.6	99.8	98.8	98.9	101.1
106	99.2	99.1	99.4	98.2	98.5	100.6
107	98.7	98.8	99.0	97.6	97.7	100.2
112	97.5	98.4	98.2	96.1	96.3	98.8
100	100.0	100.0	100.0	100.0	100.0	100.0
103	99.5	99.4	99.2	100.0	99.8	99.4
104	101.1	100.9	101.0	101.8	101.3	100.6
101	101.2	100.5	101.0	101.7	101.5	100.5
102	101.4	100.6	101.3	102.1	101.5	100.2
101	101.5	100.4	101.4	101.9	101.4	100.0
101	101.4	100.6	101.7	101.8	100.9	99.3
102	101.0	100.1	101.2	101.4	100.6	98.9
103	100.7	99.5	100.8	100.9	100.3	98.6
104	99.4	98.8	99.5	99.3	99.3	98.5

(table continues next page)

Table A.4 Employment and wage developments in the United States, software workers and other major occupational categories, 1999-2006 *(continued)*

Occupational category/ period	Total employment	Annual mean wage	Annual base wages (current dollars)				
			10th percentile	25th percentile	Median wage	75th percentile	90th percentile
Production							
1999Q4	12,620,920	25,400	14,070	17,090	22,360	31,070	42,160
2000Q4	12,400,080	26,450	14,540	17,830	23,390	32,380	43,810
2001Q4	11,270,210	27,600	15,110	18,630	24,570	33,790	45,480
2002Q4	10,726,670	28,190	15,440	18,970	25,000	34,480	46,580
2003Q2	10,488,450	28,710	15,670	19,380	25,630	35,100	47,190
2003Q4	10,246,130	28,930	15,770	19,550	25,910	35,270	47,370
2004Q2	10,128,200	29,280	15,950	19,780	26,300	35,660	47,840
2004Q4	10,194,200	29,480	16,040	19,910	26,480	35,840	48,250
2005Q2	10,249,220	29,890	16,240	20,170	26,850	36,250	48,910
2006Q2	10,268,510	30,480	16,580	20,550	27,360	36,980	49,810
Transportation and material moving							
1999Q4	9,538,820	24,630	12,730	15,590	21,220	29,990	40,600
2000Q4	9,592,740	25,630	13,200	16,230	21,940	31,230	42,270
2001Q4	9,410,660	26,560	13,670	16,820	22,800	32,520	43,710
2002Q4	9,395,000	27,220	14,100	17,140	23,180	33,030	44,610
2003Q2	9,414,920	27,600	14,240	17,390	23,520	33,440	44,820
2003Q4	9,361,690	27,630	14,230	17,440	23,610	33,470	44,760
2004Q2	9,581,320	27,880	14,340	17,630	23,880	33,780	44,940
2004Q4	9,597,380	28,250	14,450	17,830	24,240	34,170	45,370
2005Q2	9,594,920	28,820	14,690	18,180	24,750	34,730	46,260
2006Q2	9,647,730	29,460	14,960	18,570	25,300	35,430	47,680

n.a. = not available

a. Data for "all occupations" category available only from 2001 onward. Index data for this category is 2001 = 100.

Note: The data in this table include all released surveys from the Bureau of Labor Statistics (BLS), Occupational Employment Statistics (OES) program from 1999 to 2006 under the Office of Management and Budget's Standard Occupational Classification (SOC) system. The time-series in this table is irregular due to changes in the methodology used by the BLS in conducting this survey, which has for some years been released semiannually and for others annually.

Sources: Bureau of Labor Statistics, Occupational Employment Statistics, available at www.bls.gov/oes; Bureau of Labor Statistics, Consumer Price Indexes, US City Average, All Items, Seasonally Adjusted, Series ID: CUSR0000SA0, www.bls.gov/cpi.

Employment and real base wage index (1999Q4 = 100, CPI deflated)

Total employment	Annual mean wage	10th percentile	25th percentile	Median wage	75th percentile	90th percentile
100	100.0	100.0	100.0	100.0	100.0	100.0
98	100.7	99.9	100.9	101.1	100.7	100.5
89	103.1	101.9	103.4	104.3	103.2	102.4
85	103.0	101.8	103.0	103.8	103.0	102.5
83	103.9	102.3	104.2	105.3	103.8	102.9
81	103.7	102.1	104.2	105.5	103.4	102.3
80	103.0	101.3	103.4	105.1	102.6	101.4
81	102.3	100.5	102.7	104.4	101.7	100.9
81	102.2	100.2	102.5	104.3	101.3	100.7
81	100.2	98.4	100.4	102.2	99.4	98.7
100	100.0	100.0	100.0	100.0	100.0	100.0
101	100.6	100.2	100.6	100.0	100.7	100.6
99	102.3	101.9	102.4	102.0	102.9	102.2
98	102.6	102.8	102.0	101.4	102.2	102.0
99	103.0	102.8	102.5	101.8	102.5	101.4
98	102.2	101.8	101.9	101.3	101.6	100.4
100	101.2	100.7	101.1	100.6	100.7	98.9
101	101.1	100.0	100.8	100.7	100.4	98.5
101	101.6	100.2	101.3	101.3	100.6	98.9
101	99.9	98.1	99.5	99.6	98.7	98.1

References

Note: All websites were accessed on September 28, 2007.

Aldonas, Grant, Robert Z. Lawrence, and Matthew J. Slaughter. 2007. *Succeeding in the Global Economy—A New Policy Agenda for the American Worker.* Washington: Financial Services Forum.

American Electronics Association. 2005. *Losing the Competitive Advantage? The Challenge for Science and Technology in the United States.* Washington.

American Electronics Association. 2007. *We Are Still Losing the Competitive Advantage—Now Is the Time to Act.* Washington.

Anderson, Stuart. 2006. Should Congress Raise the H-1B Cap? Testimony before the House Subcommittee on Immigration, Citizenship, Refugees, Border Security, and International Law, March 30, Washington.

ATSCO (Association of Technology Staffing Companies). 2006. *Half of IT Employees Considering Changing Jobs as Pay Skyrockets* (November 15). Available at www.atsco.org.

ATSCO (Association of Technology Staffing Companies). 2007. *Research Reveals 32% Jump in IT Work Permits Issued in Past Year* (February 1). Available at www.atsco.org.

Auriol, Laudeline. 2007. *Labour Market Characteristics and International Mobility of Doctorate Holders: Results for Seven Countries.* OECD Science, Technology and Industry Working Paper 2007/2. Paris: Organization for Economic Cooperation and Development.

Autor, David H., Frank Levy, and Richard Murnane. 2001. *The Skill Content of Recent Technological Change, An Empirical Exploration.* NBER Working Paper 8337. Cambridge, MA: National Bureau of Economic Research.

Baily, Martin N., and Jacob F. Kirkegaard. Forthcoming. *Pension Reforms in Rich Countries under Demographic Stress.* Washington: Peterson Institute for International Economics. Draft on file with author.

Balatova, Jeanne. 2007. *The "Brain Gain" Race Begins with Foreign Students.* Washington: Migration Policy Institute (January 1). Available at ww.migrationinformation.org.

Bassanini, Andrea, and Stefano Scarpetta. 2001. *Does Human Capital Matter for Growth in the OECD Countries? Evidence from Pooled Mean-Group Estimates.* OECD Economics Department Working Paper 282. Paris: Organization for Economic Cooperation and Development.

BLS (Bureau of Labor Statistics). 2007. *Changes in the Composition of Labor for BLS Multifactor Productivity Measures, 2005.* Washington. Available at www.bls.gov.

Borjas, George J. 1999. The Economic Analysis of Immigration. In *Handbook of Labor Economics* 3, ed. Orley C. Ashenfelter and David Card. Amsterdam: Elsevier.

Borjas, George J. 2001. *Does Immigration Grease the Wheels of the Labor Market?* Brookings Papers on Economic Activity 69-133. Washington: Brookings Institution.

Borjas, George J. 2003. The Labor Demand Curve is Downward Sloping: Re-examining the Impact of Immigration on the Labor Market. *Quarterly Journal of Economics* (November): 1335–74.

Bound, John, and Sarah Turner. 2002. *Closing the Gap or Widening the Divide: The Effects of the G.I. Bill and World War II on the Educational Outcomes of Black Men.* NBER Working Paper 9044. Cambridge, MA: National Bureau of Economic Research.

Burda, Michael. 2006a. The Ruins of Humbolt—Restoring German Higher Education. *Berlin Journal* (Fall): 46-49. Berlin: American Academy.

Burda, Michael. 2006b. German Universities at the Cross-roads. Humbolt University. Photocopy.

Camota, Steven A. 1997. The Effect of Immigrants on Earnings of Low-Skilled Native Workers: Evidence from the June 1991 Current Population Survey. *Social Science Quarterly* 78 (June): 417–31.

Chinese Academy of Social Sciences. 2007. *Blue Book on Global Politics and Security.* Beijing.

Clark, Stephen. 2007. *Immigration Laws and Policies: Immigration Points Systems—Canada.* Report to Congress (April). Washington: Law Library of Congress.

Cohen, David, and Marcelo Soto. 2007. Growth and Human Capital: Good Data, Good Results. *Journal of Economic Growth* 12, no. 1 (March): 51–76.

CEA (Council of Economic Advisers). 2007. *Immigration's Economic Impact.* White Paper (June). Washington.

de la Fuente, Angel, and Antonio Ciccone. 2003. *Human Capital in a Global Knowledge-Based Economy.* Report prepared for the Directorate General for Employment and Social Affairs of the European Commission. Available at http://pareto.uab.es.

DeLong, J. Bradford, Claudia Goldin, and Lawrence F. Katz. 2003. Sustaining U.S. Economic Growth. In *Agenda for the Nation,* ed. H. Aaron, J. Lindsay, and P. Nivola. Washington: Brookings Institution Press.

Duke University, Master of Engineering Management Program, and University of California Berkeley School of Information. 2007. *America's New Immigrant Entrepreneurs* (January 4). Available at http://memp.pratt.duke.edu.

Dumont, Jean-Christophe, and George Lemaitre. 2005. *Counting Immigrants and Expatriates in the OECD Countries: A New Perspective.* OECD Social, Employment and Migration Working Paper 25. Paris: Organization for Economic Cooperation and Development.

Eggertsson, Thrainn. 1972. *Economic Aspects of Higher Education Taken under the World War II Bill of Rights.* Final Report. Springfield, VA: National Technical Information Service.

European Commission. 2007. *E-Skills for the 21st Century: Fostering Competitiveness, Growth and Jobs.* COM (2007) 496 Final. Brussels.

GAO (Government Accountability Office). 2005. *Department of Homeland Security, U.S. Citizenship and Immigration Services: Allocation of Additional H-1B Visas Created by the H-1B Visa Reform Act of 2004.* Document B-296402 sent to US Senate and House Judiciary Committees, May 18. Washington.

GAO (Government Accountability Office). 2006. *H-1B Visa Program—More Oversight by Labor Can Improve Compliance with Program Requirements.* GAO Publication 06-901T. Washington.

German Marshall Fund. 2006. *Perspectives on Trade and Poverty Reduction.* 2006 Survey Results. Available at www.gmfus.org.

Goldin, Claudia. 2001. The Human Capital Century and American Leadership: Virtues of the Past. *Journal of Economic History* 61: 263–91.

Goldin, Claudia, and Lawrence F. Katz. 2003. *The 'Virtues' of the Past: Education in the First*

Hundred Years of the New Republic. NBER Working Paper 9958. Cambridge, MA: National Bureau of Economic Research.

Gonzalez, Emilio T. 2007. Statement of the Director of USCIS Regarding Proposal to Adjust the Immigration Benefit Application and Petition Fee Schedule before the House Subcommittee on Immigration, Citizenship, Refugees, Border Security and International Law, February 14, Washington.

Hewitt Associates LLC. 2006. *Global Salary Planning Report 2005 and 2006.* Available at www.hewittassociates.com.

Hira, Ron. 2007. *Outsourcing America's Technology and Knowledge Jobs.* EPI Briefing Paper 187 (March). Washington: Economic Policy Institute.

Hira, Ron, and Anil Hira. 2005. *Outsourcing America.* New York: AMACOM Books.

INS (US Immigration and Naturalization Service). 2000a. *Leading Employers of Specialty Occupation Workers (H-1B): October 1999 to February 2000.* Washington.

INS (US Immigration and Naturalization Service). 2000b. *Report on Characteristics of Specialty Occupation Workers (H-1B): May 1998 to July 1999.* Washington. Available on web page "Reports and Studies/H-1B: Specialty Occupation Workers Statistical Reports" at www.uscis.gov.

INS (US Immigration and Naturalization Service). 2002a. *Report on Characteristics of Specialty Occupation Workers (H-1B): Fiscal Year 2000.* Washington. Available on web page "Reports and Studies/H-1B: Specialty Occupation Workers Statistical Reports" at www.uscis.gov.

INS (US Immigration and Naturalization Service). 2002b. *Report on Characteristics of Specialty Occupation Workers (H-1B): Fiscal Year 2001.* Washington. Available on web page "Reports and Studies/H-1B: Specialty Occupation Workers Statistical Reports" at www.uscis.gov.

Institute for International Education. 2006. *Open Doors 2006—Report on International Educational Exchange.* New York. Available at http://opendoors.iienetwork.org.

Kauffman Foundation. 2006. *Kauffman Index of Entrepreneurial Activity—National Report 1996–2005.* Kansas City.

Kirkegaard, Jacob F. 2005. *Outsourcing and Skill Imports: Foreign High-Skilled Workers on H-1B and L-1 Visas in the United States.* Working Paper 05-15. Washington: Institute for International Economics.

Lawrence, Robert Z. Forthcoming. *Blue-Collar Blues: Is Trade to Blame?* Policy Analyses in International Economics. Washington: Peterson Institute for International Economics.

Leamer, E. 1984. *Sources of International Comparative Advantage: Theory and Evidence.* Cambridge, MA: MIT Press

Levy, Frank, and Richard J. Murnane. 1992. U.S. Earnings Levels and Earnings Inequality: A Review of Recent Trends and Proposed Explanations. *Journal of Economic Literature* 30, no. 3 (September).

Levy, Frank, and Peter Temin. 2007. *Inequality and Institutions in 20th Century America.* NBER Working Paper 13106. Cambridge, MA: National Bureau of Economic Research.

Lipset, Seymour Martin. 1996. *American Exceptionalism.* New York: W. W. Norton and Company.

Lowell, B. Lindsay. 2000. *H-1B Temporary Workers: Estimating the Population.* Washington: Institute for the Study of International Migration, Georgetown University.

Lowell, B. Lindsay. 2007. *Trends in International Migration Flows and Stocks, 1975–2005.* OECD Social, Employment and Migration Working Paper 58. Paris: Organization for Economic Cooperation and Development.

Lowell, B. Lindsay, and Bryan Christian. 2000. *Employers of Foreign Temporary Workers (H-1Bs) in Information Technology.* Washington: Institute for the Study of International Migration, Georgetown University.

Mann, Catherine L. 2003. *Globalization of IT Services and White Collar Jobs: The Next Wave of Productivity Growth.* Policy Briefs in International Economics 03-11. Washington: Institute for International Economics.

Mann, Catherine L, with Jacob F. Kirkegaard. 2006. *Accelerating the Globalization of America—The Role of Information Technology.* Washington: Institute for International Economics.

McKinsey Global Institute. 2005. *The Emerging Global Labor Market: Part II—The Supply of Offshore Talent in Services.* San Francisco: McKinsey and Company.

Miano, John. 2007. *Low Salaries for Low Skills—Wages and Skill Levels for H-1B Computer Workers, 2005.* Center for Immigration Studies Backgrounder (April). Washington: Center for Immigration Studies.

Ministry of Statistics and Programme Implementation. 2005. *Results from the 61st National Sample Survey—Report #517: Status of Education and Vocational Training in India 2004-05.* New Delhi: Government of India.

Murphy, Kara. 2006. *France's New Law: Control Immigration Flows, Court the Highly Skilled.* Washington: Migration Policy Institute (November 1). Available at www.migrationinformation.org.

NASSCOM (National Association of Software and Service Companies). 2007. *Indian IT Industry Fact Sheet.* Available at www.nasscom.in.

National Academy of Sciences. 2005. *Policy Implications of International Graduate Students and Postdoctoral Scholars in the United States.* Washington: The National Academies Press.

National Academy of Sciences. 2007. *Rising above the Gathering Storm—Energizing and Employing America for a Brighter Economic Future.* Washington: The National Academies Press.

National Bureau of Statistics of China. 2005. *China Statistical Yearbook 2005.* Beijing.

National Center for Education Statistics. 2004. *Highlights from the Trends in International Mathematics and Science Study (TIMSS) 2003.* Washington: US Department of Education.

National Research Council. 2001. *Building a Workforce for the Information Economy.* Washington: The National Academies Press.

National Science Foundation. 1998. *Statistical Profiles of Foreign Doctoral Recipients in Science and Engineering: Plans to Stay in the United States.* NSF Publication 99-304. Washington.

National Science Foundation. 2005. *2003 College Graduates in the US Workforce: A Profile,* NSF Publication 06-304. Washington.

National Science Foundation. 2007. *Why Did They Come to the United States? A Profile of Immigrant Scientists and Engineers.* NSF Publication 07-324. Washington.

National Venture Capital Association. 2007. *American Made—The Impact of Immigrants, Entrepreneurs and Professionals on US Competitiveness.* Arlington, VA.

NCEE (National Center on Education and the Economy). 2007. *Tough Choices or Tough Times—Report of the New Commission on Skills of The American Workforce.* Washington.

OECD/Statistics Canada. 2005. *Learning a Living—First Results from the Adult Literacy and Life Skills Survey.* Paris: Organization for Economic Cooperation and Development.

OECD (Organization for Economic Cooperation and Development). 2006a. *Live Longer, Work Longer.* Paris.

OECD (Organization for Economic Cooperation and Development). 2006b. *International Migration Outlook 2006.* Paris.

OECD (Organization for Economic Cooperation and Development). 2007a. *OECD Employment Outlook 2007.* Paris.

OECD (Organization for Economic Cooperation and Development). 2007b. *Economic Survey of the United States 2007.* Paris.

OECD (Organization for Economic Cooperation and Development). 2007c. *International Migration Outlook 2007.* Paris.

OECD (Organization for Economic Cooperation and Development). 2007d. *Education at a Glance 2007: OECD Indicators.* Paris.

Office of Immigration Statistics. 2006. *U.S. Legal Permanent Residents: 2005.* Annual Flow Report (April). Washington: US Department of Homeland Security.

Office of Immigration Statistics. 2007. *U.S. Legal Permanent Residents: 2006.* Annual Flow Report (March). Washington: US Department of Homeland Security.

Orrenius, Pia M., and Madeline Zavodny. 2007. Does Immigration Affect Wages? A Look at Occupation-Level Evidence. *Labour Economics* 14: 757–73. Amsterdam: Elsevier.

Ottaviano G., and G. Peri. 2006. *Rethinking the Effects of Immigration on Wages.* NBER Working Paper 12497. Cambridge, MA: National Bureau of Economic Research.

Passell, Jeffrey. 2007. *Unauthorized Migrants in the United States: Estimates, Methods, and Characteristics.* OECD Social, Employment and Migration Working Paper 57. Paris: Organization for Economic Cooperation and Development.

Scheve, Kenneth F., and Matthew J. Slaughter. 2001. *Globalization and the Perceptions of American Workers.* Washington: Institute for International Economics.

Smith, James P. 2006. Immigrants and the Labor Market. *Journal of Labour Economics* 24, no. 2: 203–33. Chicago, IL: University of Chicago Press.

Splitz-Oener, Alexandra. 2007. Technical Change, Job Tasks, and Rising Educational Demands: Looking Outside the Wage Structure. *Journal of Labor Economics* 24 (April): 235–70. Chicago, IL: University of Chicago Press.

US Census Bureau. 2007. *Statistical Abstract of the United States: 2007.* Washington. Available at www.census.gov/compendia/statab.

USCIS (US Citizenship and Immigration Service). 2006a. *Characteristics of Specialty Occupation Workers (H-1B): Fiscal Year 2004.* Washington: Department of Homeland Security. Available on web page "Reports and Studies/H-1B: Specialty Occupation Workers Statistical Reports" at www.uscis.gov.

USCIS (US Citizenship and Immigration Service). 2006b. *Characteristics of Specialty Occupation Workers (H-1B): Fiscal Year 2005.* Washington: Department of Homeland Security. Available on web page "Reports and Studies/H-1B: Specialty Occupation Workers Statistical Reports" at www.uscis.gov.

US Department of Homeland Security. 2000. *2000 Yearbook of the Immigration and Naturalization Service.* Washington.

US Department of Homeland Security. 2001. *2001 Yearbook of the Immigration and Naturalization Service.* Washington.

US Department of Homeland Security. 2002. *2002 Yearbook of Immigration Statistics.* Washington.

US Department of Homeland Security. 2003a. *2003 Yearbook of Immigration Statistics.* Washington.

US Department of Homeland Security, Office of Immigration Statistics. 2003b. *Characteristics of Specialty Occupation Workers (H-1B): Fiscal Year 2002.* Washington. Available on web page "Reports and Studies/H-1B: Specialty Occupation Workers Statistical Reports" at www.uscis.gov.

US Department of Homeland Security. 2004a. *2004 Yearbook of Immigration Statistics.* Washington.

US Department of Homeland Security, Office of Immigration Statistics. 2004b. *Characteristics of Specialty Occupation Workers (H-1B): Fiscal Year 2003.* Washington. Available on web page "Reports and Studies/H-1B: Specialty Occupation Workers Statistical Reports" at www.uscis.gov.

US Department of Homeland Security. 2005. *2005 Yearbook of Immigration Statistics.* Washington.

US Department of Homeland Security. 2006. *2006 Yearbook of Immigration Statistics.* Washington.

US Department of State, Bureau of Consular Affairs. 2000. *Report of the Visa Office 2000.* Washington.

US Department of State, Bureau of Consular Affairs. 2001. *Report of the Visa Office 2001.* Washington.

US Department of State, Bureau of Consular Affairs. 2002. *Report of the Visa Office 2002.* Washington.

US Department of State, Bureau of Consular Affairs. 2003. *Report of the Visa Office 2003.* Washington.

US Department of State, Bureau of Consular Affairs. 2004. *Report of the Visa Office 2004.* Washington.

US Department of State, Bureau of Consular Affairs. 2005. *Report of the Visa Office 2005.* Washington.

US Department of State, Bureau of Consular Affairs. 2006. *Report of the Visa Office 2006.* Washington.

White, Lisa. 2007. *Immigration Law and Policies: Immigration Points Systems—Australia.* Report to Congress (April). Washington: Law Library of Congress.

Zavodny, Madeline. 2003. The H-1B Program and Its Effects on Information Technology Workers. *Economic Review* (3rd quarter). Atlanta: Federal Reserve Bank of Atlanta.

Index

adjustment of status, 34, 34f. *See also* legal permanent resident (LPR) status
   cut-off dates for, 36–38
administrative delays in visa processing, 37–38, 81
age distribution
   educational attainment, 6, 7f, 8, 9n, 10, 79, 92t–93t
   international comparison of, 11, 12f
   science and engineering workforce, 23, 25, 25n, 26f
age groups, perception of globalization by, 14, 14n
American Competitiveness in the 21st Century Act, 34n
American exceptionalism, 15, 19
antifraud fee, 78
application process, changes to, 37–38
auction system, H-1B visa, 77–78
Australia
   foreign-born population, 16
   foreign student retention program, 28
   free trade agreement with US, 76, 76n, 87
   immigration policy, 27, 28f, 29n
Austria, 16

baby boomer generation, retirement of, 6, 7f, 8n, 15, 57, 79
blue card (European Union), 30
brain chain, 89
brain drain, 3n, 30n
brain flows, 3n
Brin, Sergey, 25b
Bureau of Labor Statistics (BLS), 5n, 6n, 33

Occupational Employment Statistics, 64, 64n, 66, 106t–119t

Canada
   foreign-born population, 16
   foreign student retention program, 28, 29n
   free trade agreement with US, 87–88, 88n
   immigration policy, 27, 28f, 29n
   skill levels, 80
Chile, free trade agreement with US, 76, 76n, 87, 88n
China
   cut-off dates for, 36–38
   foreign student retention rate, 23, 80
   "green passage" policy, 31, 80
   immigrants from, 23n
   immigration policy, 30–31
   L-1 visa issuance, 39–40
   per-country limit, 36, 81, 83
   skill level, 15n
citizenship, access to, differences between, 16
competition
   for foreign students, 20, 20n, 27–29, 80, 85
   for high-skilled workers, 26–31
   labor market, 57–58
computer sciences. *See also* IT services sector; software workers
   students in, 23n
Congress
   immigration "grand compromise," 83
   request for visa program data, 40, 50, 81

corruption, 37n
Current Population Survey, 6n, 59n
cut-off dates, for adjustment of status,
    36–38

demand
    for high-skilled workers, 3, 82
    for legal permanent resident status,
        36–37
demand-supply mismatch, quotas and,
    75–77, 85
demographic skills dividend, 8
Department of Homeland Security, US
Citizenship and Immigration Service,
    36–38
Department of Labor
    Employment and Training Administra-
        tion, 55
    law enforcement by, 73, 84–85, 85n
Department of State, 36
Durbin, Richard J., 40, 50, 50n, 81, 85n, 86,
    86n

earnings. See wage(s)
economic growth, effect of skill level on, 6
educational attainment, 6–15
    age distribution, 6, 7f, 8, 9n, 10, 79,
        92t–93t
    international comparison of, 11, 12f
    earnings inequality and, 9, 9n, 14, 57
    effect on economic growth, 6
    foreign-born population, 17, 17n, 18f, 19,
        19n, 29, 30f
    international comparison of, 11, 12f,
        15–19, 79–80
    projections for, 9n, 9–10, 10f
    as skill point, 75
    stagnation in, 20, 21f, 79
    statistics on, 7f, 92t–93t
educational institutions, H-1B visa
    issuance, 53
educational threshold, 6n
education policy
    importance of, 2
    interaction with immigration policy, 3
education reform
    effect on skill level, 3, 57, 82
    need for, 15
effective skill effects, 5n
efficiency versus equity trade-off, 4, 55–58,
    75–77
employers
    matching high-skilled workers with,
        74–78
    visa number restrictions on, 86
Employment and Training Administration
    (ETA), 55

employment data. See also unemployment
    rate
    by occupational categories, 106t–119t
    software workers, 59, 60f, 61, 62b–63b, 71,
        106t–119t
    visa issuance compared to, 33, 49–52, 72
employment-related immigration, 26
    categories of, 34n
    data on, lack of, 33, 41, 90
    international comparison of, 27, 28f
    permanent (See legal permanent resident
        [LPR] status)
    quotas on (See per-country limits;
        quotas)
    temporary (See L-1 visa program;
        H-1B visa program)
entrepreneurial zeal, inflow of, 24b–25b, 80
equal opportunity maxim, educational
    attainment and, 11
equity versus efficiency trade-off, 4, 55–58,
    75–77
European Union. See also specific country
    blue card, 30
    foreign-born population, 16–17, 17f
    foreign student retention programs, 29,
        29n
    immigration policy, 27, 28f, 29–30, 30f
    IT sector, 72n
executives, foreign transfer of, 74. See also
    L-1 visa program

family-related immigration, 26, 74
    dominance of, 27, 28f, 33, 80, 83
    per-country limits for, 36
    unused quota diverted to employment-
        related visas, 34n
fees
    H-1B visa, 77–78, 78n, 82
    IT visa (proposed), 89
    premium processing, 37, 37n, 77
F-1 optional practical training (OPT), 28n,
    47, 47n, 85
foreign-born, definition of, 16, 16n
foreign labor certification (FLC), 39n, 50n,
    55–56, 73
    abolishment of, 83–84
    for points systems, 75
    prevailing wage, 73n, 73–74
foreign students
    competition for, 20, 20n, 27–29, 80, 85
    effect of 9/11 on, 20, 20n, 80
    retention of, 22–23, 23n, 28–29, 48, 80, 85
    in science and engineering, 20, 22, 22f,
        24b, 80
    temporary work visa programs for, 20,
        22f, 26, 74

US share of, 11*n*–12*n*, 14*n*, 22, 24*b*, 27–29, 80
France, 29
free trade agreements (FTAs), 76, 87–90. *See also specific agreement*

Gates, Bill, 25*b*
GATS (General Agreement on Trade in Services) visa, 88, 88*n*
Germany
  foreign student retention program, 29, 29*n*
  skill level, 13
GI Bill. *See* Servicemen's Readjustment Act of 1944
globalization, skill superiority and, 2, 13, 13*n*, 14–15, 57
Grassley, Charles, 40, 50, 50*n*, 81, 85*n*, 86, 86*n*
green card. *See* legal permanent resident (LPR) status
"green passage" (China), 31, 80
growth theory, 2

H-1B visa program, 43–53
  auction system, 77–78
  costs of, 77–78, 78*n*, 82
  eligibility criteria, 39*n*
  employment rate compared with, 49–52, 72
  Indian nationals, 47*b*, 44*t*–45*t*, 48–53, 51*t*–52*t*, 77–78, 81–82
  labor certification (*See* foreign labor certification (FLC))
  lottery, 78
  quotas (*See* per-country limits; quotas)
  reform recommendations, 84–90
    role of, 2
  science and engineering stu dents, 48
  software workers, 58, 61, 71*n*
  statistics on, 43, 46*b*–47*b*, 44*t*–45*t*, 78, 95*t*–98*t*
  top users of, 50, 51*t*–52*t*, 81–82,100*t*–105*t*
  user share restrictions, 86
  wage criteria (*See* prevailing wage)
high-skilled immigration. *See also specific visa categories*
  effects on US workers, 55, 57–58
  versus regular immigration, 3–4, 55
  welfare economics issues in, 4, 55–58, 75–77
high-skilled workers
  definition of, 1*n*
  demand for, 3
  global competition for, 26–31
  immobility of, 23

matching employers with, 74–78
  numbers forecast, 9
  science and engineering, 20–26
  software sector (*See* software workers)
  unemployment rate, 14*n*, 57
humanitarian immigration, 26, 74
IBM, 62*b*
illegal immigration, 16, 16*n*, 26, 74
immigrants, definition of, 16
immigration. *See also* high-skilled immigration
  classification of, 26
  illegal, 16, 16*n*, 74
  international comparison of, difficulties with, 16
  large-scale, 15
  managed, 27, 29–30, 75, 80
Immigration and Nationality Act (1990), 34, 36, 75
immigration data
  congressional request for, 40, 50, 81
  lack of, 33, 41, 90
  linking labor-market outcomes with, 33
  publishing of, 90
immigration policy
  by category, 27, 28*f*, 74
  conflicting and changing, 1–2
  importance of, 2
  interaction with education policy, 3
  international comparison of, 27, 28*f*
  labor-market matching, 74–78
  restrictive, negative effects of, 4
immigration reform, 36, 79–90
  need for, 1–2, 15, 57, 79–82
  politics of, 4, 81, 83
  recommendations, 82–90
immigration size effects, 15
immigration system, 33–53
  administrative delays, 37–38, 81
  agencies involved in, 36
  purposes of, 3–4, 55
India
  business model, 50, 86–88
  cut-off dates for, 36–38
  foreign student retention rate, 22
  H-1B visa issuance, 46*b*, 44*t*–45*t*, 48–53, 51*t*–52*t*, 77–78, 81–82
  High Level Committee on Indian Diaspora, 89
  immigrants from, 23*n*
  immigration agreement with US, 86–89
  immigration policy, 30–31
  L-1 visa issuance, 39–42, 41*t*–42*t*, 81–82, 84
  National Association of Software and Service Companies (NASSCOM), 89

per-country limit, 36, 81, 83
skill levels, 15n
software sector, 58–74, 62b–63b, 72–73, 81
Infosys, 50–51, 53t, 77, 87n
Institute for International Education, 20n
intracompany transfers, 74. *See also* L-1
    visa program
Iraq, 3n
IT services sector. *See also* software workers
    business model, 50, 86–88
    H-1 visa issuance, 44t–45t, 48–53,
        51t–52t, 78, 81
    offshoring in, 62b, 72
    US-India immigration agreement for,
        86–89
IT visa (proposed), 87–89

Japan
    immigration policy, 29–30
    skill level, 80
July 2007 Visa Bulletin (US State
    Department), 37–38

Karnik, Kiran, 89
Kauffman Index of Entrepreneurial
    Activity, 24b

labor capacity, effects of high-skilled
    immigration on, 55
labor certification. *See* foreign labor
    certification (FLC)
labor composition index, 5n
labor condition applications (LCAs), 71n.
    See also foreign labor certification (FLC)
labor force
    compositional improvement of,
        8–9, 56–57
    effect of retirement on, 6, 7f, 8n, 57
    international comparison of, 14
    qualitative improvement in, 5–6, 7f, 8
labor-market competition, protecting US
    workers against, 57–58
labor-market matching, 74–78
labor-market outcomes, linking visa data
    with, 33
labor-market testing, 56
large-scale immigration, 15
law enforcement, of prevailing wage
    criteria, 73, 84–85, 85n
legal permanent resident (LPR) status,
    33–38
    adjustment of status to, 36, 53, 80–81
    demand for, 36–37
    policy decisions on, 1–2, 36
    reform recommendations, 83–84
    role of, 2, 80–81

statistics, 34, 34f
system bottlenecks, 37–38, 81
lifelong learning, 6n
lottery, H-1B visa, 78
L-1 visa program, 39–42, 74
    eligibility criteria, 39n, 56, 56n
    Indian nationals, 39–42, 41t–42t,
        81–82, 84
    reform recommendations, 84
    software sector, 58
    statistics, 39, 40f
    top 25 users, 40–42, 41t–42t, 81–82
    user share restrictions, 86
L-1 Visa Reform Act (2004), 39n

Madison, James, 1
managed immigration, 27, 29–30, 75, 80
Mexico
    cut-off dates for, 36–37
    free trade agreement with US, 87–88, 88n
    immigration policy, 30
Microsoft, 62b–63b
multifactor productivity (MFP), 5n, 6

National Academy of Sciences, 25n, 29n
National Association of Software
    and Service Companies (NASSCOM),
    89
National Science Foundation, 8n, 20n, 22,
    27, 59n
    Science and Engineering Indicators, 25n
National Venture Capital Association,
    4, 24b
new arrivals, for permanent residency,
    34, 35f
New Zealand
    foreign-born population, 16
    immigration policy, 27, 28f
North American Free Trade Agreement
    (NAFTA), 87–88, 88n

occupational categories, 61, 61n, 66n
    employment rate by, 106t–119t
    wage distribution by, 67, 68t–69t, 70f,
        106t–119t
Occupational Employment Statistics
    (OES), 64, 64n, 66, 106t–119t
OECD countries. *See also specific country*
    de facto time-series data, 11, 12f
    educational attainment in, 15–19
    foreign-born population, 16–17, 17f
    immigration policy, 27, 28f, 80
    labor-market testing, 56
    skill level in, 13–14, 57, 80
OECD Database on Foreign-born and
    Expatriates, 16

OECD *International Migration Outlook 2007*, 56
offshoring, 62*b*, 72
Omidyar, Pierre, 25*b*
Omnibus Appropriations Act (FY2005), 39*n*, 73*n*, 77
optional practical training (OPT), 28*n*, 47, 47*n*, 85
Oracle, 62*b*

Patni Computer Systems, Inc., 73–74
per-country limits, 36. *See also* quotas
  exemptions from, 83–84
permanent immigration, 26. *See also* legal permanent resident (LPR) status
  international comparison of, 27, 28*f*
  reform recommendations, 83–84
Philippines
  cut-off dates for, 36–38
  per-country limit, 81, 83
points systems, 29, 29*n*, 74–75
politics of immigration reform, 4, 81, 83
Portman, Robert, 87*n*
premium processing fee, 37, 37*n*, 77
prevailing wage, 73–74
  definition of, 73*n*
  enforcement of, 73, 84–85, 85*n*
Programmers Guild, 62*b*
project-based onsite delivery model, 50, 86–88
publishing of immigration data, 90

quotas, 1, 34, 34*n*, 48, 75, 78*n*. *See also* per-country limits
  abolishment of, 85
  versus actual number granted, 43, 81
  negative effects of, 75–77
  reform of, 83–84

Real ID Act, 34*n*
refugees, 26
rent seeking, 58, 58*n*
  H-1B visa program and, 77–78, 82
  wage distribution and, 71
  researchers, foreign transfer of, 74. *See also* L-1 visa program
retirement
  baby boomer generation, 6, 7*f*, 8*n*, 15, 57, 79
  international comparison of, 14
retirement age, 8*n*, 25*n*
retraining fee, 77
Russia, 13*n*, 13–14, 80

science and engineering (S&E), 20–26
  foreign students, 20, 22, 22*f*, 24*b*, 80

retention of, 22–23, 23*n*, 48
  immigration issues related to, 25–27
  US resident-born students, 20, 21*f*, 80
  workforce age distribution, 23, 23*n*, 25, 25*n*, 26*f*
Servicemen's Readjustment Act of 1944 (GI Bill), 3, 3*n*
Silicon Valley, 24*b*
Singapore, free trade agreement with US, 76, 76*n*, 87, 88*n*
skill level
  determinants of, 5
  effect of education reform on, 3, 5
  effect on economic growth, 6
  international comparison of, 13–14, 57, 79–80
  rising, 7*f*, 8
  stagnation of, 8–9, 56–57, 79
  of unauthorized immigrants, 26*n*
skills capacity, maximum, 11
skill shortages, forecasting of, 2, 9*n*, 9–10, 10*f*, 14
skills points, 29, 29*n*, 74–75
skill superiority, globalization and, 13, 13*n*, 14–15, 57
software workers, 58–74, 82
  composition of, 71–72
  definition of, 59*n*
  employment rate, 59, 60*f*, 61, 62*b*–63*b*, 71, 106*t*–119*t*
  international comparison of, 72–73
  supply of, 58*n*
  US-India immigration agreement for, 86–89
  wages, 62*b*, 64, 64*n*, 65*t*, 66*n*, 66–67, 67*n*, 106*t*–119*t*
  effect of immigrants on, 71*n*, 71–72, 82
Solow, Robert, 2
South Korea
  foreign student retention rate, 23
  skill level, 13, 80
Standard Occupational Classification (SOC), 61, 61*n*
  employment rate by, 106*t*–119*t*
  wage distribution by, 67, 68*t*–69*t*, 70*f*, 106*t*–119*t*
State Department, *Visa Bulletin*, 36–38
students. *See* foreign students
substitutability, between immigrants and native workers, 57*n*
Switzerland, 16

Taiwan, 23
Tata Consultancy Services, 86, 87*n*
temporary immigration, 26, 39–53. *See also* H-1B visa program; L-1 visa program

adjustment to permanent residency (*See* adjustment of status)
immigration reform and, 36
as primary gateway of entry, 36, 81, 85
for students, 20, 22*f*, 26, 74
terrorist attacks (9/11), numbers of foreign students and, 20, 20*n*, 80
tertiary education. *See* educational attainment
trade agreements, immigration provisions in, 76, 87, 87*n*, 87–90. *See also specific agreement*
trade liberalization, skill superiority and, 13, 13*n*, 14–15, 57

unemployment rate
high-skilled workers, 14*n*, 57
software workers, 59, 59*n*, 60*f*, 61, 71
visa issuance compared with, 49–52
UNESCO, 11
United Kingdom
foreign student retention program, 29, 29*n*, 85
immigration policy, 29*n*
software workers in, 72–73
US Census Bureau, 9–10, 14*n*
Current Population Survey, 6*n*, 59*n*
US Citizenship and Immigration Service (USCIS), 36–38, 43, 44*t*, 49
US foreign-born population, 15
educational attainment, 17, 17*n*, 18*f*, 19, 19*n*
US resident population
educational attainment of, 6–15, 57
government labor protection for, 57–58
immobility of, 23, 57
maximum skills capacity of, 11
skill superiority of, 13, 13*n*, 57
substitutability between immigrants and, 57*n*
universities
foreign students at (*See* foreign students)
quality differences among, 11

venture capital–backed companies, immigrant-founded, 24*b*–25*b*
Visa Bulletin (US State Department), 36–38
visa expiration, individuals remaining after, 26*n*
visa hoarding, 76–77
visa mark-up, 89
visa petitions, administrative delays in, 37–38, 81

wage(s)
prevailing (*See* prevailing wage)
software workers, 62*b*, 64, 64*n*, 65*t*, 66*n*, 66–67, 67*n*, 106*t*–119*t*

effect of immigrants on, 71*n*, 71–72, 82
wage distribution
educational attainment and, 9, 9*n*, 14, 57
by occupational categories, 67, 68*t*–69*t*, 70*f*, 106*t*–119*t*
welfare economics, 4, 55–58, 75–77
Wipro, 87*n*

Other Publications from the Peterson Institute

* = out of print

Economic Sanctions Reconsidered (2 volumes)
Economic Sanctions Reconsidered:
Supplemental Case Histories
Gary Clyde Hufbauer, Jeffrey J. Schott, and
Kimberly Ann Elliott
1985, 2d ed. Dec. 1990   ISBN cloth 0-88132-115-X
ISBN paper 0-88132-105-2
Economic Sanctions Reconsidered: History
and Current Policy   Gary Clyde Hufbauer,
Jeffrey J. Schott, and Kimberly Ann Elliott
December 1990   ISBN cloth 0-88132-140-0
ISBN paper 0-88132-136-2
Pacific Basin Developing Countries: Prospects
for Economic Sanctions Reconsidered: History
and Current Policy   Gary Clyde Hufbauer,
Jeffrey J. Schott, and Kimberly Ann Elliott
December 1990   ISBN cloth 0-88132-140-0
ISBN paper 0-88132-136-2
Pacific Basin Developing Countries: Prospects
for the Future*   Marcus Noland
January 1991   ISBN cloth 0-88132-141-9
ISBN paper 0-88132-081-1
Currency Convertibility in Eastern Europe*
John Williamson, editor
October 1991   ISBN 0-88132-128-1
International Adjustment and Financing: The
Lessons of 1985-1991*   C. Fred Bergsten, editor
January 1992   ISBN 0-88132-112-5
North American Free Trade: Issues and
Recommendations*
Gary Clyde Hufbauer and Jeffrey J. Schott
April 1992   ISBN 0-88132-120-6
Narrowing the U.S. Current Account Deficit*
Alan J. Lenz/*June 1992*   ISBN 0-88132-103-6
The Economics of Global Warming
William R. Cline/*June 1992* ISBN 0-88132-132-X
US Taxation of International Income:
Blueprint for Reform   Gary Clyde Hufbauer,
assisted by Joanna M. van Rooij
October 1992   ISBN 0-88132-134-6
Who's Bashing Whom? Trade Conflict
in High-Technology Industries
Laura D'Andrea Tyson
November 1992   ISBN 0-88132-106-0
Korea in the World Economy*
Il SaKong
January 1993   ISBN 0-88132-183-4
Pacific Dynamism and the International
Economic System*
C. Fred Bergsten and Marcus Noland, editors
May 1993   ISBN 0-88132-196-6
Economic Consequences of Soviet
Disintegration*   John Williamson, editor
May 1993   ISBN 0-88132-190-7
Reconcilable Differences? United States-Japan
Economic Conflict*
C. Fred Bergsten and Marcus Noland
June 1993   ISBN 0-88132-129-X
Does Foreign Exchange Intervention Work?
Kathryn M. Dominguez and Jeffrey A. Frankel
September 1993   ISBN 0-88132-104-4

Sizing Up U.S. Export Disincentives*
J. David Richardson
September 1993   ISBN 0-88132-107-9
NAFTA: An Assessment Gary Clyde
Hufbauer and Jeffrey J. Schott/*rev. ed.*
October 1993   ISBN 0-88132-199-0
Adjusting to Volatile Energy Prices
Philip K. Verleger, Jr.
November 1993   ISBN 0-88132-069-2
The Political Economy of Policy Reform
John Williamson, editor
January 1994   ISBN 0-88132-195-8
Measuring the Costs of Protection
in the United States   Gary Clyde Hufbauer
and Kimberly Ann Elliott
January 1994   ISBN 0-88132-108-7
The Dynamics of Korean Economic
Development*   Cho Soon
March 1994   ISBN 0-88132-162-1
Reviving the European Union*
C. Randall Henning, Eduard Hochreiter, and
Gary Clyde Hufbauer, editors
April 1994   ISBN 0-88132-208-3
China in the World Economy
Nicholas R. Lardy
April 1994   ISBN 0-88132-200-8
Greening the GATT: Trade, Environment,
and the Future   Daniel C. Esty
July 1994   ISBN 0-88132-205-9
Western Hemisphere Economic Integration*
Gary Clyde Hufbauer and Jeffrey J. Schott
July 1994   ISBN 0-88132-159-1
Currencies and Politics in the United States,
Germany, and Japan   C. Randall Henning
September 1994   ISBN 0-88132-127-3
Estimating Equilibrium Exchange Rates
John Williamson, editor
September 1994   ISBN 0-88132-076-5
Managing the World Economy: Fifty Years
after Bretton Woods   Peter B. Kenen, editor
September 1994   ISBN 0-88132-212-1
Reciprocity and Retaliation in
U.S. Trade Policy
Thomas O. Bayard and Kimberly Ann Elliott
September 1994   ISBN 0-88132-084-6
The Uruguay Round: An Assessment*
Jeffrey J. Schott, assisted by
Johanna W. Buurman
November 1994   ISBN 0-88132-206-7
Measuring the Costs of Protection in Japan*
Yoko Sazanami, Shujiro Urata,
and Hiroki Kawai
January 1995   ISBN 0-88132-211-3
Foreign Direct Investment in the
United States, 3d ed.,
Edward M. Graham and Paul R. Krugman
January 1995   ISBN 0-88132-204-0
The Political Economy of Korea-United
States Cooperation*
C. Fred Bergsten and Il SaKong, editors
February 1995   ISBN 0-88132-213-X

International Debt Reexamined*
William R. Cline
February 1995 ISBN 0-88132-083-8
American Trade Politics, 3d ed.
I. M. Destler
April 1995 ISBN 0-88132-215-6
Managing Official Export Credits:
The Quest for a Global Regime*
John E. Ray
July 1995 ISBN 0-88132-207-5
Asia Pacific Fusion: Japan's Role in APEC*
Yoichi Funabashi
October 1995 ISBN 0-88132-224-5
Korea-United States Cooperation in the New
World Order* C. Fred Bergsten and Il SaKong, eds.
February 1996 ISBN 0-88132-226-1
Why Exports Really Matter!* ISBN 0-88132-221-0
Why Exports Matter More!* ISBN 0-88132-229-6
J. David Richardson and Karin Rindal
July 1995; February 1996
Global Corporations and National Governments
Edward M. Graham
May 1996 ISBN 0-88132-111-7
Global Economic Leadership and the Group of
Seven C. Fred Bergsten and C. Randall Henning
May 1996 ISBN 0-88132-218-0
The Trading System after the Uruguay Round*
John Whalley and Colleen Hamilton
July 1996 ISBN 0-88132-131-1
Private Capital Flows to Emerging Markets
after the Mexican Crisis*
Guillermo A. Calvo, Morris Goldstein,
and Eduard Hochreiter
September 1996 ISBN 0-88132-232-6
The Crawling Band as an Exchange Rate Regime:
Lessons from Chile, Colombia, and Israel
John Williamson
September 1996 ISBN 0-88132-231-8
Flying High: Liberalizing Civil Aviation
in the Asia Pacific*
Gary Clyde Hufbauer and Christopher Findlay
November 1996 ISBN 0-88132-227-X
Measuring the Costs of Visible Protection
in Korea* Namdoo Kim
November 1996 ISBN 0-88132-236-9
The World Trading System: Challenges Ahead
Jeffrey J. Schott
December 1996 ISBN 0-88132-235-0
Has Globalization Gone Too Far?
Dani Rodrik
March 1997 ISBN paper 0-88132-241-5
Korea-United States Economic Relationship*
C. Fred Bergsten and Il SaKong, editors
March 1997 ISBN 0-88132-240-7
Summitry in the Americas: A Progress Report
Richard E. Feinberg
April 1997 ISBN 0-88132-242-3
Corruption and the Global Economy
Kimberly Ann Elliott
June 1997 ISBN 0-88132-233-4

Regional Trading Blocs in the World
Economic System Jeffrey A. Frankel
October 1997 ISBN 0-88132-202-4
Sustaining the Asia Pacific Miracle:
Environmental Protection and Economic
Integration Andre Dua and Daniel C. Esty
October 1997 ISBN 0-88132-250-4
Trade and Income Distribution
William R. Cline
November 1997 ISBN 0-88132-216-4
Global Competition Policy
Edward M. Graham and J. David Richardson
December 1997 ISBN 0-88132-166-4
Unfinished Business: Telecommunications
after the Uruguay Round
Gary Clyde Hufbauer and Erika Wada
December 1997 ISBN 0-88132-257-1
Financial Services Liberalization in the WTO
Wendy Dobson and Pierre Jacquet
June 1998 ISBN 0-88132-254-7
Restoring Japan's Economic Growth
Adam S. Posen
September 1998 ISBN 0-88132-262-8
Measuring the Costs of Protection in China
Zhang Shuguang, Zhang Yansheng,
and Wan Zhongxin
November 1998 ISBN 0-88132-247-4
Foreign Direct Investment and Development:
The New Policy Agenda for Developing
Countries and Economies in Transition
Theodore H. Moran
December 1998 ISBN 0-88132-258-X
Behind the Open Door: Foreign Enterprises
in the Chinese Marketplace
Daniel H. Rosen
January 1999 ISBN 0-88132-263-6
Toward A New International Financial
Architecture: A Practical Post-Asia Agenda
Barry Eichengreen
February 1999 ISBN 0-88132-270-9
Is the U.S. Trade Deficit Sustainable?
Catherine L. Mann
September 1999 ISBN 0-88132-265-2
Safeguarding Prosperity in a Global Financial
System: The Future International Financial
Architecture, Independent Task Force Report
Sponsored by the Council on Foreign Relations
Morris Goldstein, Project Director
October 1999 ISBN 0-88132-287-3
Avoiding the Apocalypse: The Future
of the Two Koreas Marcus Noland
June 2000 ISBN 0-88132-278-4
Assessing Financial Vulnerability: An Early
Warning System for Emerging Markets
Morris Goldstein, Graciela Kaminsky,
and Carmen Reinhart
June 2000 ISBN 0-88132-237-7
Global Electronic Commerce: A Policy Primer
Catherine L. Mann, Sue E. Eckert, and Sarah
Cleeland Knight
July 2000 ISBN 0-88132-274-1

The WTO after Seattle   Jeffrey J. Schott, editor
July 2000   ISBN 0-88132-290-3
Intellectual Property Rights in the Global Economy   Keith E. Maskus
August 2000   ISBN 0-88132-282-2
The Political Economy of the Asian Financial Crisis   Stephan Haggard
August 2000   ISBN 0-88132-283-0
Transforming Foreign Aid: United States Assistance in the 21st Century
Carol Lancaster
August 2000   ISBN 0-88132-291-1
Fighting the Wrong Enemy: Antiglobal Activists and Multinational Enterprises
Edward M. Graham
September 2000   ISBN 0-88132-272-5
Globalization and the Perceptions of American Workers   Kenneth Scheve/Matthew J. Slaughter
March 2001   ISBN 0-88132-295-4
World Capital Markets: Challenge to the G-10
Wendy Dobson and Gary Clyde Hufbauer, assisted by Hyun Koo Cho
May 2001   ISBN 0-88132-301-2
Prospects for Free Trade in the Americas
Jeffrey J. Schott
August 2001   ISBN 0-88132-275-X
Toward a North American Community: Lessons from the Old World for the New
Robert A. Pastor
August 2001   ISBN 0-88132-328-4
Measuring the Costs of Protection in Europe: European Commercial Policy in the 2000s
Patrick A. Messerlin
September 2001   ISBN 0-88132-273-3
Job Loss from Imports: Measuring the Costs
Lori G. Kletzer
September 2001   ISBN 0-88132-296-2
No More Bashing: Building a New Japan–United States Economic Relationship
C. Fred Bergsten, Takatoshi Ito, and Marcus Noland
October 2001   ISBN 0-88132-286-5
Why Global Commitment Really Matters!
Howard Lewis III and J. David Richardson
October 2001   ISBN 0-88132-298-9
Leadership Selection in the Major Multilaterals   Miles Kahler
November 2001   ISBN 0-88132-335-7
The International Financial Architecture: What's New? What's Missing?   Peter Kenen
November 2001   ISBN 0-88132-297-0
Delivering on Debt Relief: From IMF Gold to a New Aid Architecture
John Williamson and Nancy Birdsall, with Brian Deese
April 2002   ISBN 0-88132-331-4
Imagine There's No Country: Poverty, Inequality, and Growth in the Era of Globalization   Surjit S. Bhalla
September 2002   ISBN 0-88132-348-9

Reforming Korea's Industrial Conglomerates
Edward M. Graham
January 2003   ISBN 0-88132-337-3
Industrial Policy in an Era of Globalization: Lessons from Asia
Marcus Noland and Howard Pack
March 2003   ISBN 0-88132-350-0
Reintegrating India with the World Economy
T. N. Srinivasan and Suresh D. Tendulkar
March 2003   ISBN 0-88132-280-6
After the Washington Consensus: Restarting Growth and Reform in Latin America   Pedro-Pablo Kuczynski and John Williamson, editors
March 2003   ISBN 0-88132-347-0
The Decline of US Labor Unions and the Role of Trade   Robert E. Baldwin
June 2003   ISBN 0-88132-341-1
Can Labor Standards Improve under Globalization?
Kimberly Ann Elliott and Richard B. Freeman
June 2003   ISBN 0-88132-332-2
Crimes and Punishments? Retaliation under the WTO   Robert Z. Lawrence
October 2003   ISBN 0-88132-359-4
Inflation Targeting in the World Economy
Edwin M. Truman
October 2003   ISBN 0-88132-345-4
Foreign Direct Investment and Tax Competition
John H. Mutti
November 2003   ISBN 0-88132-352-7
Has Globalization Gone Far Enough? The Costs of Fragmented Markets
Scott Bradford and Robert Z. Lawrence
February 2004   ISBN 0-88132-349-7
Food Regulation and Trade: Toward a Safe and Open Global System
Tim Josling, Donna Roberts, and David Orden
March 2004   ISBN 0-88132-346-2
Controlling Currency Mismatches in Emerging Markets
Morris Goldstein and Philip Turner
April 2004   ISBN 0-88132-360-8
Free Trade Agreements: US Strategies and Priorities   Jeffrey J. Schott, editor
April 2004   ISBN 0-88132-361-6
Trade Policy and Global Poverty
William R. Cline
June 2004   ISBN 0-88132-365-9
Bailouts or Bail-ins? Responding to Financial Crises in Emerging Economies
Nouriel Roubini and Brad Setser
August 2004   ISBN 0-88132-371-3
Transforming the European Economy
Martin Neil Baily and Jacob Kirkegaard
September 2004   ISBN 0-88132-343-8
Chasing Dirty Money: The Fight Against Money Laundering
Peter Reuter and Edwin M. Truman
November 2004   ISBN 0-88132-370-5

The United States and the World Economy:
Foreign Economic Policy for the Next Decade
C. Fred Bergsten
January 2005   ISBN 0-88132-380-2
**Does Foreign Direct Investment Promote
Development ?**   Theodore Moran, Edward
M. Graham, and Magnus Blomström, editors
April 2005   ISBN 0-88132-381-0
American Trade Politics, 4th ed.
I. M. Destler
June 2005   ISBN 0-88132-382-9
**Why Does Immigration Divide America?
Public Finance and Political Opposition
to Open Borders**
Gordon Hanson
August 2005   ISBN 0-88132-400-0
Reforming the US Corporate Tax
Gary Clyde Hufbauer and Paul L. E. Grieco
September 2005   ISBN 0-88132-384-5
The United States as a Debtor Nation
William R. Cline
September 2005   ISBN 0-88132-399-3
**NAFTA Revisited: Achievements
and Challenges**
Gary Clyde Hufbauer and Jeffrey J. Schott,
assisted by Paul L. E. Grieco and Yee Wong
October 2005   ISBN 0-88132-334-9
**US National Security and Foreign Direct
Investment**
Edward M. Graham and David M. Marchick
May 2006   ISBN 0-88132-391-8
          ISBN 978-0-88132-391-7
**Accelerating the Globalization of America:
The Role for Information Technology**
Catherine L. Mann, assisted
by Jacob Kirkegaard
June 2006   ISBN 0-88132-390-X
          ISBN 978-0-88132-390-0
Delivering on Doha: Farm Trade and the Poor
Kimberly Ann Elliott
July 2006   ISBN 0-88132-392-6
          ISBN 978-0-88132-392-4
**Case Studies in US Trade Negotiation,
Vol. 1: Making the Rules** Charan Devereaux,
Robert Z. Lawrence, and Michael Watkins
September 2006   ISBN 0-88132-362-4
          ISBN 978-0-88132-362-7
**Case Studies in US Trade Negotiation,
Vol. 2: Resolving Disputes** Charan Devereaux,
Robert Z. Lawrence, and Michael Watkins
September 2006   ISBN 0-88132-363-4
          ISBN 978-0-88132-363-2
C. Fred Bergsten and the World Economy
Michael Mussa, editor
December 2006   ISBN 0-88132-397-7
          ISBN 978-0-88132-397-9
Working Papers, Volume I
Peterson Institute
December 2006   ISBN 0-88132-388-8
          ISBN 978-0-88132-388-7

The Arab Economies in a Changing World
Marcus Noland and Howard Pack
April 2007   ISBN 978-0-88132-393-1
Working Papers, Volume II
Peterson Institute
April 2007   ISBN 978-0-88132-404-4
**Global Warming and Agriculture:
Impact Estimates by Country**
William R. Cline
July 2007   ISBN 978-0-88132-403-7
US Taxation of Foreign Income
Gary Clyde Hufbauer and Ariel Assa
October 2007   ISBN 978-0-88132-405-1
Russia's Capitalist Revolution
Anders Åslund
October 2007   ISBN 978-0-88132-409-9
Economic Sanctions Reconsidered, 3d. ed.
Gary C. Hufbauer, Jeffrey J. Schott,
Kimberly Ann Elliott, and Barbara Oegg
November 2007
          ISBN hardcover 978-0-88132-407-5
ISBN hardcover/CD-ROM 978-0-88132-408-2

SPECIAL REPORTS

1   **Promoting World Recovery: A Statement
     on Global Economic Strategy***
     by 26 Economists from Fourteen Countries
     December 1982   ISBN 0-88132-013-7
2   **Prospects for Adjustment in Argentina,
     Brazil, and Mexico: Responding
     to the Debt Crisis***
     John Williamson, editor
     June 1983   ISBN 0-88132-016-1
3   **Inflation and Indexation: Argentina,
     Brazil, and Israel***
     John Williamson, editor
     March 1985   ISBN 0-88132-037-4
4   **Global Economic Imbalances***
     C. Fred Bergsten, editor
     March 1986   ISBN 0-88132-042-0
5   **African Debt and Financing***
     Carol Lancaster and John Williamson, eds.
     May 1986   ISBN 0-88132-044-7
6   **Resolving the Global Economic Crisis:
     After Wall Street*** by Thirty-three
     Economists from Thirteen Countries
     December 1987   ISBN 0-88132-070-6
7   **World Economic Problems***
     Kimberly Ann Elliott/John Williamson, eds.
     April 1988   ISBN 0-88132-055-2
     Reforming World Agricultural Trade*
     by Twenty-nine Professionals from
     Seventeen Countries
     1988   ISBN 0-88132-088-9
8   **Economic Relations Between the United
     States and Korea: Conflict or Cooperation?***
     Thomas O. Bayard and Soogil Young, eds.
     January 1989   ISBN 0-88132-068-4

WORKS IN PROGRESS

DISTRIBUTORS OUTSIDE THE UNITED STATES

Australia, New Zealand,
and Papua New Guinea
D. A. Information Services
648 Whitehorse Road
Mitcham, Victoria 3132, Australia
Tel: 61-3-9210-7777
Fax: 61-3-9210-7788
Email: service@dadirect.com.au
www.dadirect.com.au

India, Bangladesh, Nepal, and Sri Lanka
Viva Books Private Limited
Mr. Vinod Vasishtha
4737/23 Ansari Road
Daryaganj, New Delhi 110002
India
Tel: 91-11-4224-2200
Fax: 91-11-4224-2240
Email: viva@vivagroupindia.net
www.vivagroupindia.com

Mexico, Central America, South America,
and Puerto Rico
US PubRep, Inc.
311 Dean Drive
Rockville, MD 20851
Tel: 301-838-9276
Fax: 301-838-9278
Email: c.falk@ieee.org

Asia (*Brunei, Burma, Cambodia, China,*
Hong Kong, Indonesia, Korea, Laos, Malaysia,
Philippines, Singapore, Taiwan, Thailand,
and Vietnam)
East-West Export Books (EWEB)
University of Hawaii Press
2840 Kolowalu Street
Honolulu, Hawaii 96822-1888
Tel: 808-956-8830
Fax: 808-988-6052
Email: eweb@hawaii.edu

Canada
Renouf Bookstore
5369 Canotek Road, Unit 1
Ottawa, Ontario KlJ 9J3, Canada
Tel: 613-745-2665
Fax: 613-745-7660
www.renoufbooks.com

Japan
United Publishers Services Ltd.
1-32-5, Higashi-shinagawa
Shinagawa-ku, Tokyo 140-0002
Japan
Tel: 81-3-5479-7251
Fax: 81-3-5479-7307
Email: purchasing@ups.co.jp
For trade accounts only. Individuals will find
Institute books in leading Tokyo bookstores.

Middle East
MERIC
2 Bahgat Ali Street, El Masry Towers
Tower D, Apt. 24
Zamalek, Cairo
Egypt
Tel. 20-2-7633824
Fax: 20-2-7369355
Email: mahmoud_fouda@mericonline.com
www.mericonline.com

United Kingdom, Europe
(*including Russia and Turkey*)**, Africa,**
and Israel
The Eurospan Group
c/o Turpin Distribution
Pegasus Drive
Stratton Business Park
Biggleswade, Bedfordshire
SG18 8TQ
United Kingdom
Tel: 44 (0) 1767-604972
Fax: 44 (0) 1767-601640
Email: eurospan@turpin-distribution.com
www.eurospangroup.com/bookstore

Visit our website at:
www.petersoninstitute.org
E-mail orders to:
petersonmail@presswarehouse.com